alphanumeric
iconic
arbitrary
codified

# G1

| graphics | united |
| games | first |
| geometry | one-dimensional |
| gabble | singular |
| genesis | personal |

**Subj: contemp. design, graphic**

**Lewis Blackwell and Neville Brody**

associate editors: Research Studios

assistant editor: Graham Moore

**135**

**136**

Laurence King

Published 1996 by Laurence King Publishing
an imprint of Calmann & King Ltd
71 Great Russell Street
London WC1B 3BN

A catalogue record for this book is available from the British Library.

ISBN: 1 85669 092 X

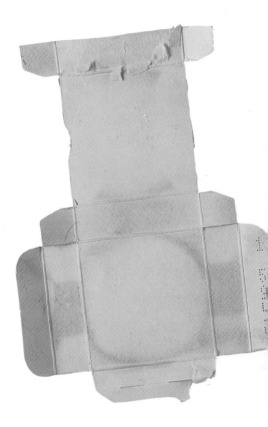

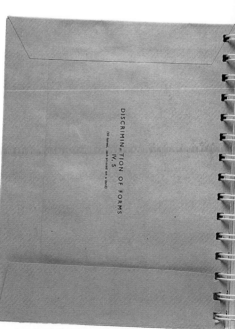

**2D** 15

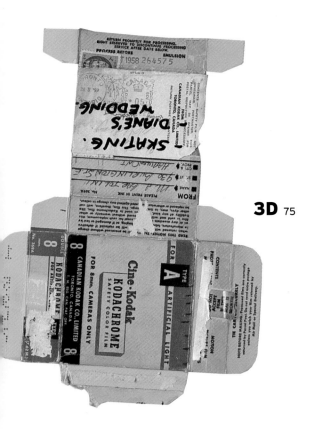

**3D** 75

**4D** 121

**IN THE BEGINNING**

| | |
|---|---|
| **Possible reasons for inclusion** | Accident |
| | You worked on the book |
| | You know somebody who worked on the book |
| | Your work was seen by somebody who worked on the book |
| | You know somebody who knows somebody who worked on the book |
| | Your work was seen by somebody who knows somebody who worked on the book |

| | |
|---|---|
| **Possibly not reasons for inclusion** | Money |
| | Membership of any organization |
| | Fame/notoriety |

This book is incomplete without your involvement.

This book needs you to play it.

This book is about how design is something much larger than what designers do.

This book is about the making of mass-communication in its most vibrant, direct form: in the graphic design we consume daily. It is a subject that is fashionable, and yet obscure. The subject is a series of questions as much as it is a body of knowledge. The questions involve the search for new fertile areas in which to plant the roots of graphic design theory. For the old roots have been damaged, torn up, ravaged by the winds of change in our visual culture.

This book shows some of the changes. It also shows some of the influences.

As new work is done, new seeds are planted – many thousands every day. Thus the visual culture grows, but to what guiding principles? Graphic design is still a discipline in search of a hard intellectual basis. In modernism it thought it had that, but as the Bauhaus ideology begat the Swiss Style which segued into the International Style, so the intellectual rigour became the label... it became a style. Now graphic designers pick'n'mix styles off the shelf, while others choose whether to see this as clever post-modern self-knowledge or a desperate lack of ideas and principles.

Faced with the decline of the dominant ideology in western design, there has been a growing pluralism. This involves integrating or exchanging existing rules with appropriations from other systems. The vernacular – that mysterious amorphous mass of "native" found material – becomes a touchstone in this process: it is perhaps seen as the empirical reality for design, how it is when designers have not been at play. Out of the modification of the "rules" of design and the codes of the vernacular emerges a new aesthetic. While it may not be founded on state-of-the-art idealism, such work has the assurance of being built on the bedrock of the vernacular. It can claim to be design that refers to life, rather than theories that are not accepted or fully shared by practitioner and reader.

Graphic design has always needed to embrace other knowledge, other experience. This may be derived from the culture of the street or of fine art and other creative disciplines, or from the deterministic nature of the technology used in putting the message across. And so our understanding of communication design cannot be left to designers and what they do. We would tend to have shorter lives if doctors only learnt from the practice and opinions of other doctors, rather than being required to take in learning from other disciplines and to listen to their patients. So it is with the design dialogue: every production is improved by knowledge that comes from outside the profession, that incorporates an awareness of who is seeing the message and the context in which it is being received.

## Vernacular

Words shift in meaning, but few more than "vernacular" when talking about design. Whereas once the term may have referred to that which was generic and untouched by professional hands, it is now taken by our contributors to refer to things that are sometimes accidental (for example, a dirty stencil or torn packaging), sometimes highly contrived but taken away from their original purpose (a haemostatic cord, soap powder packets), sometimes other. There are many examples sprinkled through the pages.

Ellen Lupton and J. Abbott Miller identified the moving target of the vernacular as being explained by the positioning of "a dominant culture against a secondary subculture. The vernacular is the Other, and any discourse has its Other." In true post-structuralist style this sets down the sense of meaning as something entirely relative, and it leaves the definition pretty wide. But it does clearly mark out the idea that "vernacular" can relate to almost anything that is outside the conventions of design as it is taught at any one time.

To fix it a little closer: the vernacular here tends to link with some sense of the native, rather than the imposed. The selections are examples of the colloquial forms of visual language, things as they are rather than as they are designed. This is still a wide definition, but it is this breadth that makes it likely that designers almost invariably stray into appropriating the vernacular whenever they challenge the notions of what is good design – whenever they dip into that Other.

The vernacular for graphic designers does not even have to be graphic, but can be anything that the designer chooses to identify. This is not quite the same as calling a dog a cat and claiming this is valid, even if it is nearly as self-centred. But whereas dogs bark and cats miaow, the vernacular for designers is whatever comes at them and influences them from outside the approved, dominant culture. The vernacular is always relative... in another time and from a different perspective it could be the clothes you are wearing, this book (the sticker sheets are appropriated from the vernacular) or the language we use. Crucially involved with the notion of the vernacular is the sense of there being no one creator, of the item being part of a generic.... ironically, designers celebrating the vernacular are admiring the absence of the designer-as-heroic-creator.

This book then is perhaps counter-productive to the discussion it wants to stimulate. Filled as it is with work submitted by graphic designers, themselves carefully chosen and then further whittled down by editors practising within the design industry, this would seem an object born reeking of hypocrisy. How can we expect readers to be less design-obsessed, to reach outward from refined design practice, when we dish up such a selection and when we are so much a part of the incestuous world ourselves!

But we have excuses. There is a logic. First consider a little biographical and procedural information, then judge.

For one thing, one of the editors is not a designer and never was. And the other one, the designer, has involved himself in new professions these past few months. Perhaps he has come to the opinion that graphic design is not as vital at present as 1) music 2) film 3) travel. He may re-read this book and wonder if it makes a case for him to return to the studio... asking the questions: What is graphic design? Is it important?

The procedure behind putting this book together was also less incestuous than one might first think. True, there was a subjective selection of designers, for the most part a list of those the editors had heard of, seen published, or had even met or worked with. These designers were invited to send in recent projects. Then most of that was sifted, put aside and, some months later, many designers were invited to update their submissions. At the same time they were asked to suggest a piece of the "vernacular" that inspired them. If that seems rather vague, it was, deliberately. But there were two good reasons why we made this final step in the collection.

Firstly, we were struck by how much use and discussion there is in design of "the vernacular". We discuss the meaning of this term separately, but here note that the theme fed straight back into our processes, prompting us to question how we developed and designed the book. We returned to those designers whose projects stood out (for initial selection reasons, see the unhelpful panel) and

asked them to respond to this theme. Most did, although again we selected from the submissions. It was a highly subjective process, involving the editors and designers sifting for items that seemed to carry the glint of something different. If we missed something, if the results are the fool's gold of graphics, then tell us. And, if you like, show us what you think is of value.

Secondly, our concentration on bringing out this theme of the vernacular gave us a means of pushing at the ideas of "high design" represented in our primary selection, probing its relationship with the everyday and with the "undesigned". Of course, these vernacular elements are now thrice-filtered through refined perceptions: first, your inadvertent endorsement in the choosing of us as editors; then our choice of the designers and their work; then their choice of the "found", of the undesigned. So what we end up with is not exactly graphic ephemera casually scraped off the street. Instead, it is a complex impression, a portrait, of the relationship between the rarified grammar of high design and the notion of the common

## Fetish

For some people, nothing can beat a good covering of rubber and leather. Graphic designers, though, get their kicks in other ways. Thick cardboard, bubble wrap, tons of print pressure applied to heavy wove paper... the delight in such objects and processes is often enough to delight... is seen to say something in itself.

At times the charm, the magic of this play with the materials and methods attains a significance that goes beyond the rational. Even if the fetish is created with very deliberate intent, this is but a framework for the quasi-religious experience it is expected to deliver: when we feel or see strange materials and treatments combined, our pleasure (if any) is not overtly intellectual, but is of the senses. Our interest is at once sensual and spiritual, we go looking for the non-rational parts of our mind to respond.

It has always been the case that materials or methods of production have been used in unusual ways to add content and value to a graphic artefact. Such innovation drives change. Aldus Manutius stood out in Renaissance Venice for his introduction of italic faces, which may have been intended as a way of imitating the calligraphic hand or may have been a way of economizing on paper, but whatever the inspiration the result was to stand apart – if only until all the other printers copied him. In that period of difference his idea would have drawn attention to the form, would have given a special reverence to his work over and above the messages carried by the type.

It is the case, of course, that most graphics are not unusual in their production, most do not innovate, but replicate. They come at us with an assumption that their processes are largely transparent, or of no significance, in the resulting statement.

In *G1* we present the awkward pieces that demand to be seen, that innovate and push the boundaries. But the result is that almost all the work in this book has some degree of self-consciousness in its presentation, inviting the viewer to look at it with fresh eyes, be surprised at the invention with which the message is transmitted. This self-consciousness at times spills over into a fetishizing of the graphic artefact: instead of the communication of a message or messages, the production of an object is the central achievement. And this object is presented as something to be admired and enjoyed for its sheer physicality.

graphic language that we share. And like any portrait, there is all kinds of subjectivity colouring it.

So we are subjective and tightly enmeshed in design issues, but we are also reaching out beyond the conventions of this industry and this culture. This is no awards annual, with its careful compromise of votes, nor is it a presentation of objects that fit a neat theory. Of course, there is some kind of underlying framework, but parts of this have been declared and you may guess at other structures, economic and social. They are infinite; there is no end to our prejudice.

If you want a grand theory, make it up. This is (just look at the work) the age of pluralism in design: you can be a modernist or a post-modernist, into deconstruction or classicism, a traditionalist in love with print culture or a techno-junkie living beyond the screen. Whichever area, it was noticeable that many of the most remarkable examples of graphic communications transform themselves from transparent carriers of information, into highly fetishistic objects (see panel). Such items may be seen as

Often this pleasure is to be taken in the making precious of commonplace materials or processes: thus the complex blind-embossing of a simple cardboard box transforms an object that might have been opened and discarded into the graphic equivalent of a jewel-encrusted chest; or the bringing together of the idea of "inflatables" with the ephemeral postcard creates a gimmick that celebrates the simple message in a way that perhaps postcards no longer can, for in their everyday-ness they have become partly invisible.

So this fetishizing can be a positive thing, re-awakening the viewer's interest... but it can also be seen as part of a more questionable movement, in which the notion of "the medium is the message" has led to self-obsessed messaging that does not communicate. The fetish graphic perhaps adorns communications with the charms of the physical world, rather than exploring and revealing the meaning available in written language.

indulgent, over-resourced, pretentious, decadent – call them what you will – but we saw them as essentially of now and included them for their topicality. Their form is representative of some condition that at least besets those of us in major cities.

We looked at these entries, trying to reject or accept nothing through conscious likes/dislikes, but instead put it in if it brought something to the party. So there is some organization to the prejudices: if anything, we acquired new prejudices in the process.

The results are a collage of different directions in graphic design. The selection eschews the established boundaries, gives no priority to any one theoretical position. This is an area in which practice is everything, albeit occasionally the work is post-rationalized. It is an area that still labours under doubts about the value of its product: today's graphics are often tomorrow's rubbish (see also panel), whereas those working in architecture or fashion, say, can be more confident that their labours result in something less transient, which is of higher perceived value in our culture.

But the lack of intellectual superstructure and cultural expectation is also an advantage for graphic production. It is perhaps the reason why graphic design can be an essential part of pop culture, rather than Culture. With graphic designers increasingly free of a monolithic rulebook (such as modernism provided),

**Tomorrow's rubbish**

The process of making precious, mass-produced graphic objects can lead to the fetish (q.v.). But it also involves another issue: the challenge to the ephemeral nature of graphics.

In seeking to give an everyday graphic artefact a value over and above that for the genre, designers are engaging with two common concerns of the 1990s: the environmental factors of production, and the fear of being lost in an ocean of other communications. While the first issue is one that many designers and their clients engage with in a somewhat worthy, and perhaps ephemeral manner, it is the second that represents the most immediate challenge. With mass-communications heaping thousands of messages on to people daily, what will make one stand out and avoid becoming waste?

And even if noticed, what gives a graphic item a value that makes it worth keeping, once read? These questions push graphics to new positions. The fear of instant death is a very real one behind the making of many communications. And, in contrast, the weight of expectation for other graphics can wear them out. A piece of direct mail, a flyer, packaging... such items slip from being created to being waste with scarcely any recognition. Meanwhile a book or a CD cover can be pored over many times – to sustain such pressure requires a certain engineering of the communication.

The movement of value in artefacts is explored at length in Michael Thompson's *Rubbish Theory: The Creation and Destruction of Value* (Oxford University Press, 1979).

## Technology (Welcome to Cybercity!)

This is another variation of the fetish (q.v.) impulse in contemporary graphics. The celebration of technology - particularly the technology of graphic production - can be seen as a major contributor to the wider excitement pertaining to the "cybercity" culture. Sometimes graphics appropriate elements and ideas from the literature of this debate, sometimes the imagery itself contributes to the cyberspace vision.

Graphics of this nature are concerned with recognizing the futuristic promise of computers, of the internet, of communities interacting in "virtual space" rather than the "real" dimensions we are used to. The language of science fiction is drawn into design, whether as sci-fi words and images, or as something more textural. Through visual and verbal reference there is the suggestion that in seeing such material one is plugging into a dialogue at the edge of our time, on the cusp of now, anticipating the future. It is, of course, no more now than anything else, but it celebrates this sense of change.

For example, the theme of electronic surveillance explored in the book *Interference* (pages 35-7) generates a graphic response of great obscurity, within which meanings can be gleaned. The strange, hidden world of the subject seems to suggest that a strange, hidden language operates around us, and ensnares us. But the devices of this book can be seen elsewhere, working to different ends, more simply celebrating graphic process/progress.

And other work can be seen to play off the near-endless repetition and variation of computer processes, making visible the machine behind the message (page 108 and elsewhere). Sometimes the sheer production values available with new technology are celebrated by images that use the latest tools to present effects not previously seen on screen or paper (page 58). If this novelty value is but gimmickry, then perhaps we should realize that gimmicks have a role in graphic design - they lock into our desire for fresh expression, for signs of progress... whatever that may be. Thus a rich montage, heavy with megabytes of information, subconsciously tells us that a lot of work is involved in putting this together, that resources were gathered to present this message... that somebody thinks it is important.

Some of the more experimental internet sites are reacting against the obsession with new technology and becoming simpler, minimal (pages 175-6). Less is more with this medium; less information works better both technically (you can download it more quickly) and as a communication (you can read it more quickly). Less information is more difficult to achieve.

The cumulative effect of all the talk of technology, and the adventure of the internet, is the vision of the online world of cyberspace, where the computer terminal is our entrance into an alternative, constructed reality. While there is argument for and against such a vision, what is clear is that it is a mere vision, and is a long way from coming to pass. But in that it projects our hopes and fears, it is very real and becomes a rich territory for image-making.

the opportunity today for graphics to be expressive is greater than for some time: the results are increasingly diverse, bizarre, ill-conceived and, occasionally, impressive. If you perceive themes that jump out of *G1*, then these are as likely to relate to issues outside design debate as within.

Look to the hidden harmonies and rhythm of music, the immersion of film, the pleasure of travel... and other contemporary media that not only provide a context for design, but can offer metaphors for the process of design. Such considerations certainly were in our minds... but the results of those impulses are here. Take them, they're yours now.

**2** Adhesive airport baggage-handling label. *54mm x 333mm.*

```
0000 337428
```

VRN 011/8    TO
MCLEAN/CMR
Y BAG01/0014

**XH 337428**

TO
# LGW

**BA 2595** 12FEB

VIA

★★★
Aeroporto ⟋⟍ Valerio Catullo di
Verona Villafranca

VIA

★★★

**XH 337428**

LGW    BA 2595
★★★
★★★
MCLEAN/CMR
VRN  12FEB / B01 /0014

# 2D

There is a conundrum here. Our theme doesn't exist and yet we all know what we are talking about. To see things in two dimensions is but a construct, and a convenience. It can also be a deceit.

We think we understand what we mean by the two-dimensional. In design studies, there are whole departments with professors dedicated to the subject. And yet nothing is two-dimensional, except in the mind. In the attempt to give order, we simplify. But everything must have some kind of mass. Every piece of paper must have some thickness, suggest some surface and that which isn't surface. And even with a television sequence or a film title, the image sits on a surface and within a physical context.

So this idea of the two-dimensional is a crude simplification. At all times, though, our imposition of this order might give a prompting for reflection: how, why and when do we attempt to bypass space and time, the third and fourth dimensions, and choose to concentrate on the two dimensions?

These questions challenge graphic designers in the creative decisions they make. When expressing their own or their clients' propagandist purposes, they do so by probing and playing with cognitive behaviour. But this activity is usually done in a fairly intuitive manner, one more attuned to previous design practice than to any great knowledge of the science of human perception.

Many graphic designers would think what they do is almost entirely two-dimensional. If only because that was the name of the course they attended. So the time their message may take to read, or the way in which it relates to the object it is on or the context of the message, is fairly haphazard. Increasingly, though, designers are waking up to the fact that graphic design is much more than just mark-making. It is perhaps particularly the designers who have experience of working across media, or across cultures, who become sensitive to how the marks have to sit somewhere – go somewhere. The marks exist in different contexts, different times and across different media.

In making our division here, our approach has been to consider how significant space and time are in the appreciation of the message. The items in this chapter are interpreted by the editors as being quickly seen communications that do not build into more complicated messages or explore three-dimensional spatial issues.

Having made these judgements, we were aware that merely by being of interest to us, the items had explored some kind of space and time. There is also the problem that what might be essentially two-dimensional seen in one instance, may also work across other dimensions at other times.

So, for example, a road sign is meant to be an almost subliminally appreciated message. We do not consciously interpret a speed limit sign, it is apprehended in a moment. However, a sequence of signs advising us of the need to slow down for an obstruction ahead exists in both space (over perhaps the several hundred metres of messaging) and in time, the seconds that elapse while we drive (at decreasing speed) through the communication.

So messages can at once be two-dimensional and part of a three- and four-dimensional experience. Under 2D, you may find an eye-catching, seductive magazine fashion photo-essay; but under 4D are photo-essays deemed to work more across time and space.

We have made our choices prompted by whether an intriguing graphic item works as a flat surface that is fairly immediately appreciated. Often it involves graphics as seductive imagery, graphics as a device to make an emotional connection, rather than as part of a more elaborate, drawn-out presentation.

You will, of course, look and decide for yourself. You can re-label those pieces you think would sit better elsewhere. In doing so, you can change the two-dimensional by playing with the three-dimensional and in so doing take it into the four-dimensional.

**3** Chopstick wrapper with chopsticks for
Oki Nami Japanese restaurant. *183mm x 36mm.*

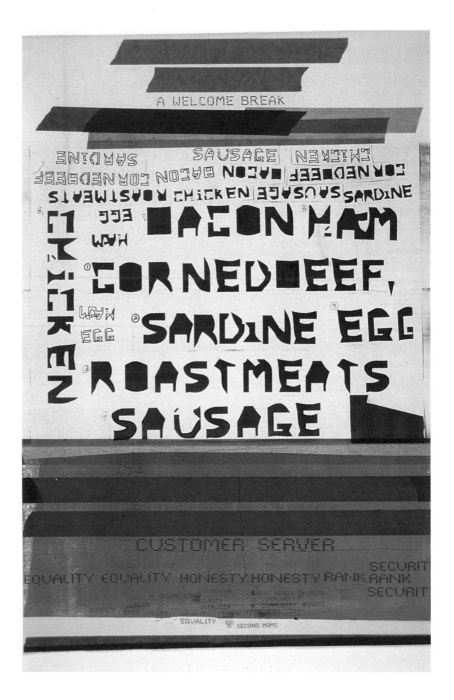

**4** Posters, non-commissioned, drawing on British café signage. *Various sizes.*

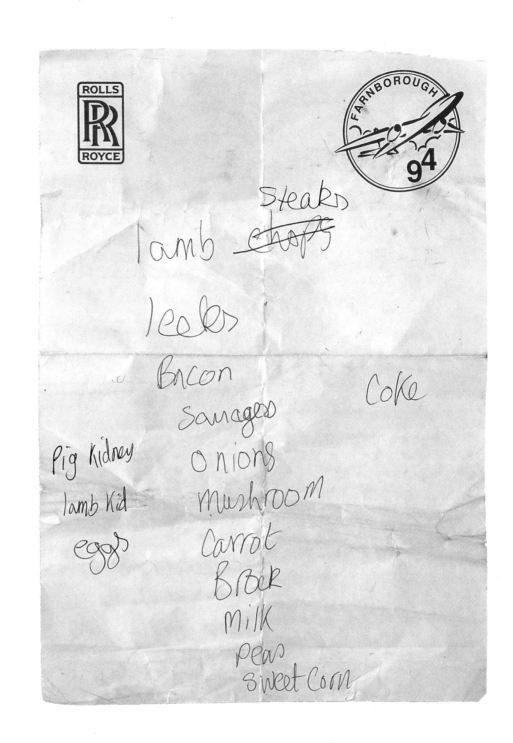

steaks
lamb ~~chops~~

leeks

Bacon                    Coke
Sausages
Pig kidney    Onions
lamb kid      mushroom
eggs          Carrot
              Brock
              milk
              Peas
              sweet corn

**5** Shopping list on Rolls Royce notepaper, elements of a recipe for an unknown meal. *145mm x 209mm.*

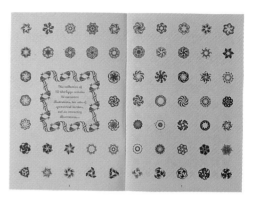

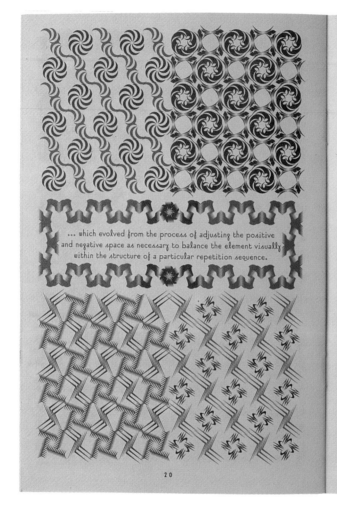

... which evolved from the process of adjusting the positive and negative space as necessary to balance the element visually within the structure of a particular repetition sequence.

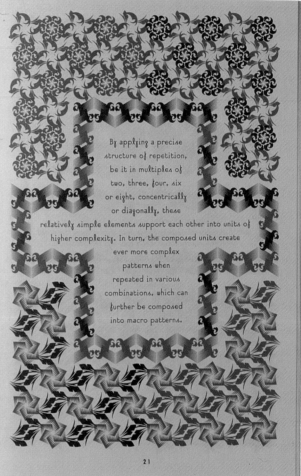

By applying a precise structure of repetition, be it in multiples of two, three, four, six or eight, concentrically or diagonally, these relatively simple elements support each other into units of higher complexity. In turn, the composed units create ever more complex patterns when repeated in various combinations, which can further be composed into macro patterns.

20

21

**6** Whirligig typeface. Illustrative elements driven by font technology to create patterns.

**7** Poster promotion of exhibition and talk by Willie Cole in San Francisco. 533mm x 838mm

**willie cole**

opening reception
thursday, march 2 6 - 8pm

"the elegba principle"
march 3 - april 29, 1995

artist's talk
saturday march 4 1pm

gallery hours
tuesday - saturday 12 - 6pm
for information, please call 415 - 495 - 7101
group tours are available upon request.
please call for an appointment.

capp street project
525 second street
[between bryant and brannan]

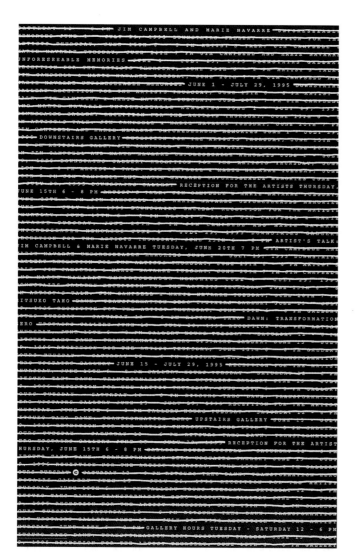

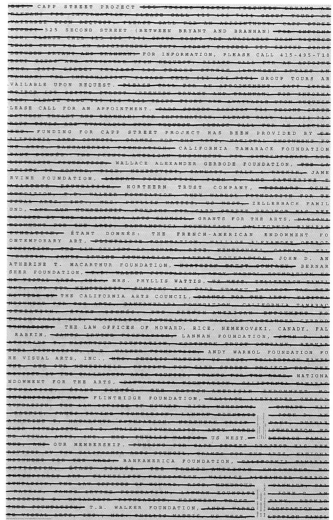

**8** Front and back of a self-mailer/poster for
Capp St Projects, an experimental arts venue.
Everything that is crossed out is revealed elsewhere.
*Flat 533mm x 838mm, folded 133mm x 210mm.*

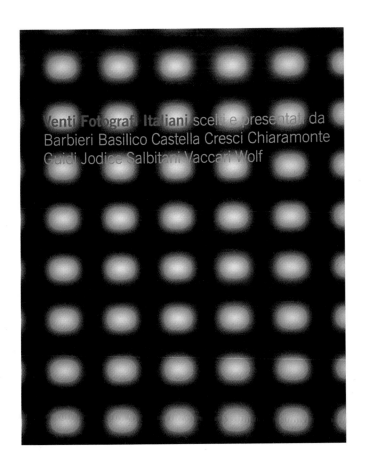

9 Front and back cover (positive/negative) of the book/catalogue Venti Fotografi Italiani.

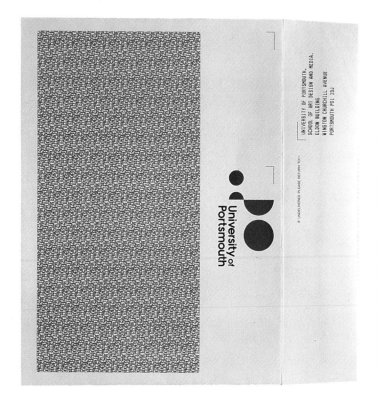
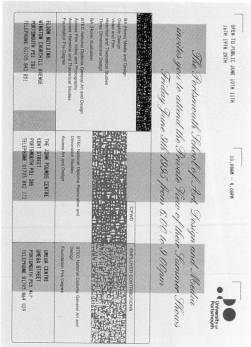
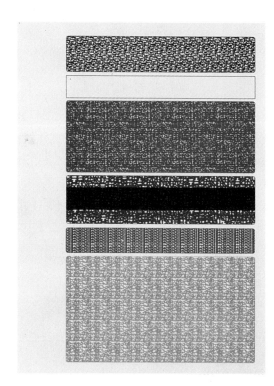
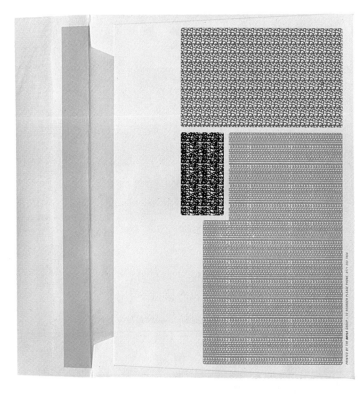

**10** Invitation card and envelope for private view at the School of Art, Design and Media, the University of Portsmouth. *197mm x 145mm.*

MARYLEBONE RD.  EUSTON ROAD

GOWER ST.

TAVISTOCK SQ.

S'HAMPTON ROW

FETTER LANE

FARRINGDON

CLERKENWELL RD.

WILLIAM CAXLON

GT. RUSSELL ST.

CITY OF LONDON

CHISWELL ST.

ST. PAUL'S CHURCH

GOUGH SQ.

FLEET STREET

PICCADILLY SQUARE

'GESTER

LUDGATE HILL  POULTRY

THAMES

RIVER

KENSINGTON GORE

Royal College
of Art

VICTORIA &
ALBERT MUSEUM

ELEPHANT
& CASTLE

H'SMITH
TERRACE

THAMES

CROMWELL RD.

RIVER

THAMES

RIVER

PECKHAM RD.

RIVER

THAMES

RIVER

Printing in London 1476-1995

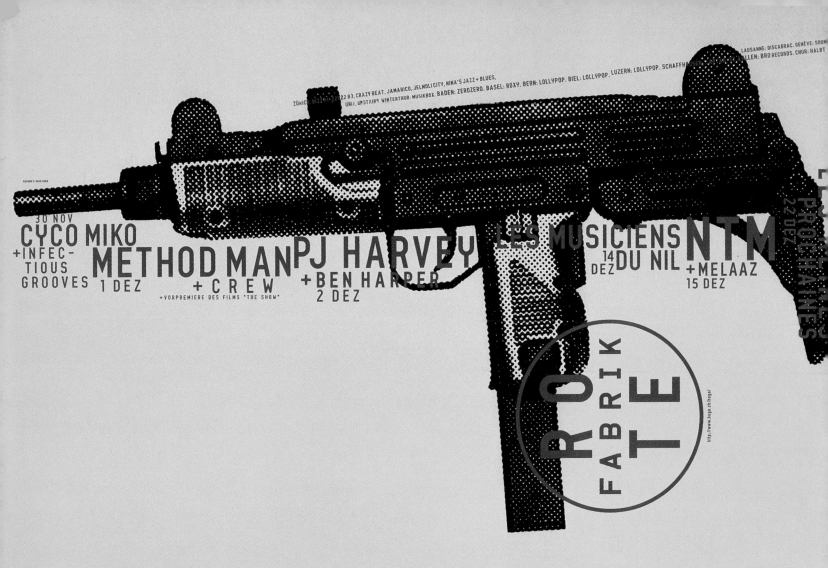

"Much of the interest of works of art lies in the ways in which they explore and modify the codes which they seem to be using." (From *Saussure* by Jonathan Culler, 1976.)

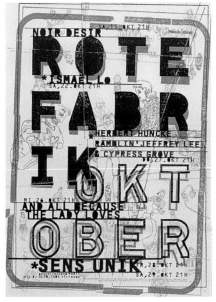

ABCDEFGHIJKLMNOPQRSTUVWXYZ

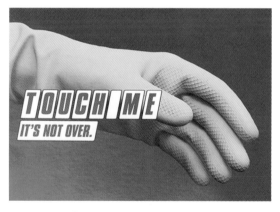

**13** Shotgun (opposite page). Font based on found sign (cover image).

**14** Postcards for the Terrence Higgins Trust HIV/AIDS campaign stressing the need for continued awareness. *150mm x 40mm*

**15** Confectionery tin for Kawai Kanyu Drops, Japan. Elliptical section with lid. *80mm x 100mm x 40mm.*

**Autechre. tri repetae.**
warplp38d. overand. rsdio.
Ae production. booth/brown. warp music/emi music. haswell. the designers republic. cunningham.
℗ & © 1995 warp records. po box 474 sheffield s1 3bw. made in england. complete with surface noise.

In 1934 the Machine Art Exhibition at the Museum of Modern Art, New York, featured objects "produced by machines for domestic, commercial, industrial and scientific purposes. Beauty – mathematical, mechanical and utilitarian – determined the choice of the objects regardless of whether their fine design was intended by artist or engineer, or merely a concomitant of machine production." (From the MOMA members' invitation.)

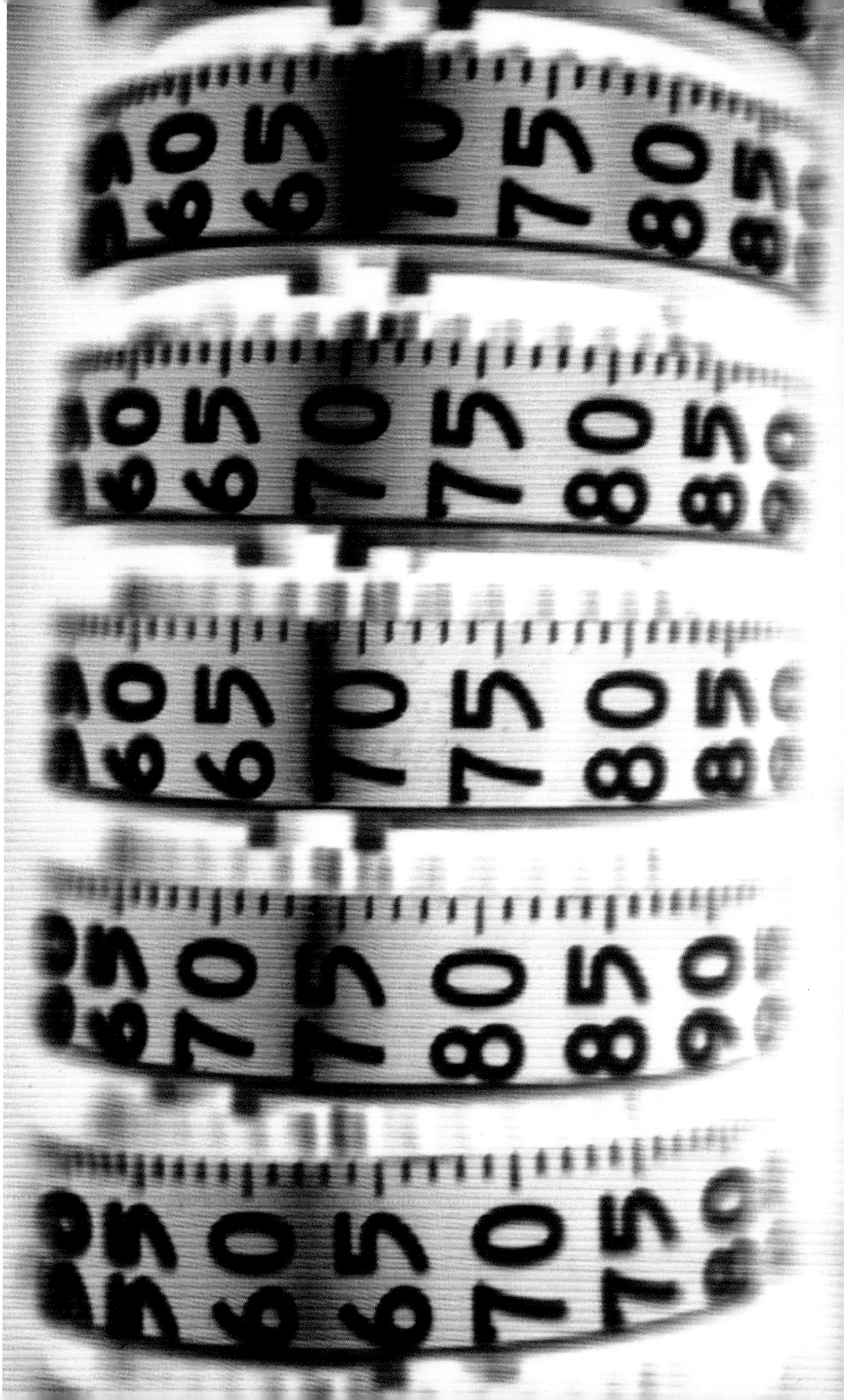

**17** Photograph, non-commissioned, of numerals from petrol pump gauges.

**18** Cover and chapter headers from the Eurobest advertising awards annual.
Images explore the differences in European electrical standards.

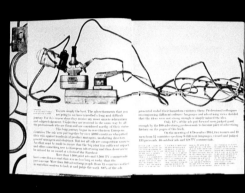

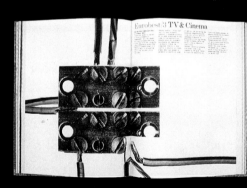

**19** Digital artwork competition poster/call for entries in US magazine Confetti. *280mm x 430mm.*

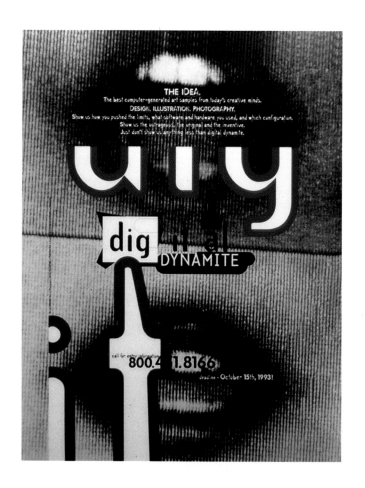

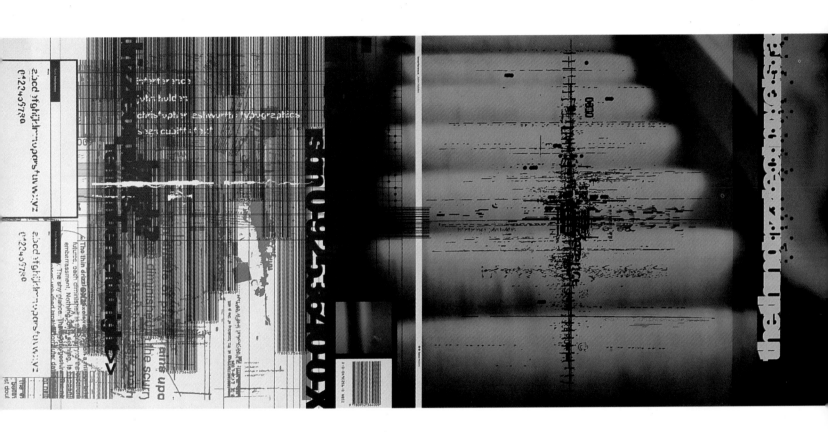

**20** Cover and spread (following pages) from Interference, a book of images by John Holden and text by Sean Cubitt, exploring the role of surveillance technology. Hardback with dustjacket. *230mm x 295mm.*

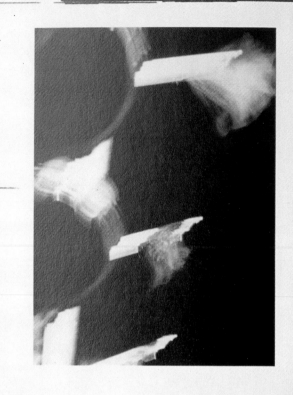

are double guaranteed. Should any item.

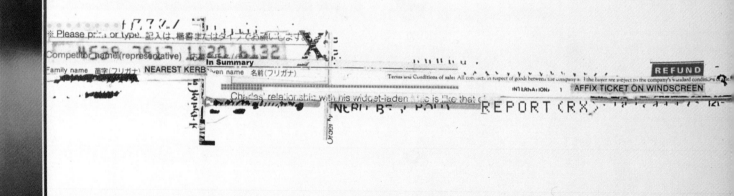

※ Please print or type. 記入は、楷書またはタイプでお願いします。

Competitor name (representative)

In Summary

Family name  苗字(フリガナ)  NEAREST KERB  Given name  名前(フリガナ)

Terms and Conditions of sales All contracts in respect of goods between the company and the buyer are subject to the company's standard conditions

INTERNATIONAL  AFFIX TICKET ON WINDSCREEN

Charles' relationship with his widget-laden shop is like that of

REPORT (RX)

REFUND

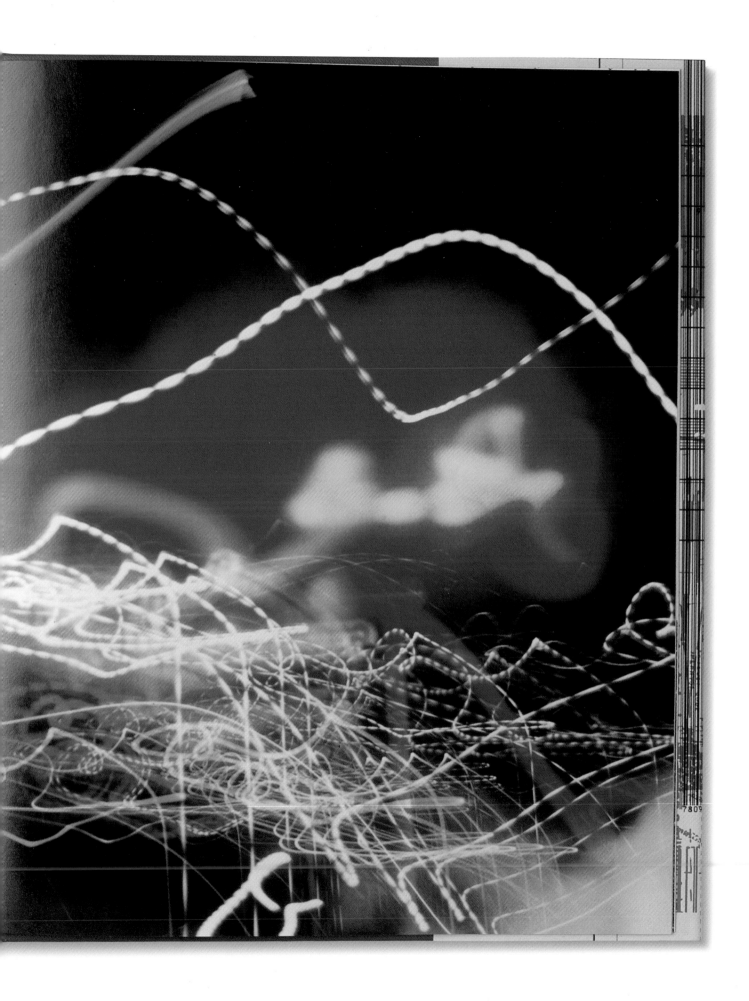

shu t up  and ride.

photographed by kevin kerslake.

sequence, photographed by brad stewart.

Noah Salasnek plays hard to get. Jake Hauswirth tries to track him down.

**21** 12" record label for Swim. Immersion Remixes Vol 1. Features manipulated image of a gas ring. *102mm diameter*.

**22** Spread from snowboard magazine Stick. Ray Gun Publishing. *255mm x 255mm*.

**23** Corroded advertisement for Coca-Cola.

Light shows, mediates and changes

**24** Set of stickers from
The Alternative Pick, a source
book of creative ideas for the
music industry. *190mm x 38mm.*

**25** Cover of Agfa type catalogue.
*155mm x 225mm.*

**26** Experimental typeface F Santo Domingo. Exploring the theme of superstition.

Hieroglyphs - picture writing - are the basis of the "western" alphabet. The letter "A" was originally a picture of the head of an ox. From being an ox, aleph in Hebrew, in the Phoenician writing system circa 1000BC, it became adopted by the Greeks as the sign for the vowel alpha... and so to the first letter of the Latin alphabet. "A" may be a vowel, but it is still a mark of visual culture.

Poster for inclusion in The Alternative Pick source book. *280mm x 430mm.*

**28** Printed letter with single pencilled initial as signature. *210mm x 297mm.*

Graham Moore
Calmann & King Limited
71 Great Russell Street
London WC1B 3BN

8 June 1995

Dear Graham Moore

Here are six examples with captions for consideration. If they are
unsuitable or you'd prefer something else don't hesitate to let me
know.

Yours sincerely

Alan Fletcher

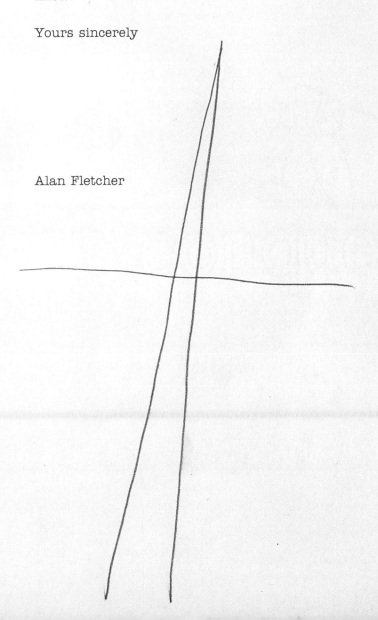

**29** Silk-screen poster. Bonjour Voisin.

**30** Cartes postales d'EuroDisney, a softback book with board sides and gates. Bound in plain card with embossed silhouette on cover. *110mm x 170mm.*

**31** Card folder for the poster museum/library Les Silos Maison du Livres et de l'Affiche, Chaumont. Contains stickers, booklets and postcards. *155mm x 120mm.*

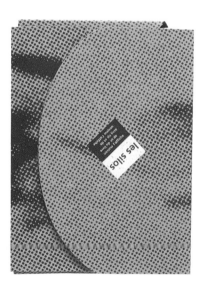 

"All language is a set of symbols whose use
among its speakers assumes a shared past."
(From *The Aleph* by Jorge Luis Borges;
translation by Norman Thomas di Giovanni.)

**32** Poster celebrating 25 years of Documenta bookshop,
Barcelona, marking signs of slow but sure development.

**33** Identity for Tragamar fish restaurant, Barcelona.
Features recycled metal sculpture. *Various dimensions.*

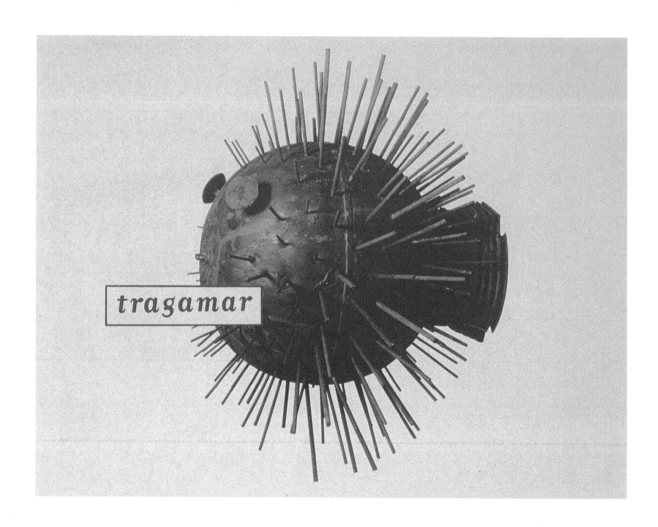

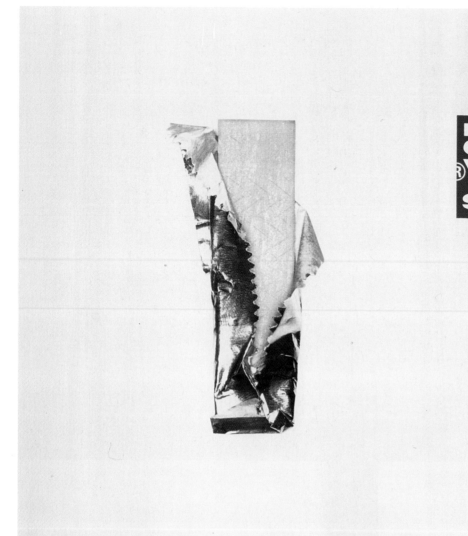

regular 505

loose 508

relaxed 517

**35** Posters for various styles of Levi Strauss jeans.

Symbols: comfort with style

**36** Three soap powder boxes.
From Czechoslovakia *144mm x 200mm x 54mm.*
From US *205mm x 285mm x 60mm.*
From India *70mm x 118mm x 22mm.*

**Symbols: cleanliness with confidence**

Advertising agencies estimate that we are exposed
to 3,000 commercial messages a day in a major city.

**37** CD packaging for Lush/4AD Records with staged photography story featuring band logo.

**38** Rump steak packaging from London butcher.

Porno
graphy
needs
you.

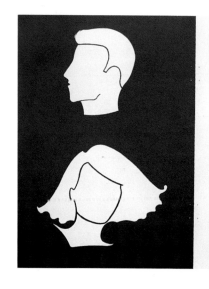

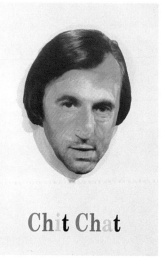

Chit Chat

**40** Poster for Time Out magazine. *500mm x 700mm.*

**41** Flyposting for launch campaign for Blah Blah Blah magazine.

**42** Advertising for Foster's Ice beer. Rejected earlier designs and final one-off poster site.

Street market

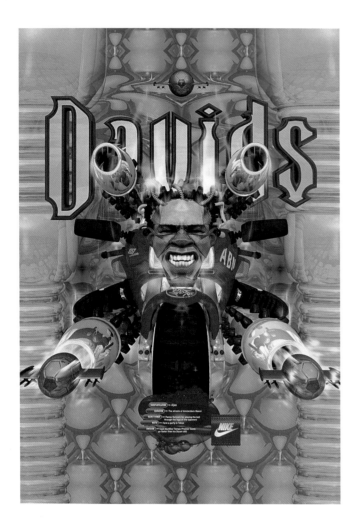

**43** Press advertisements for Nike featuring football players manipulated in three-dimensional computer environments. *Various dimensions.*

Play the game

**44** Photograph of promotion in 1950s US hi-fi store. *207mm x 254mm.*

**45** The Wild Next cover for How magazine.

**46** Stills from Lotus Software television commercial.

Technology inhabits memories and inhibits dreams. "I grew up with the clanging bells and whistles of trade show exhibits and point-of-purchase displays. I thought every basement was full of them. Martini-testers and hi-fis. This was where the working-class salesman could be artist and sculptor. Even mis-spellings are forgiven. If the stuff has some pizzazz and class, hand-rendered typography would lay the theme as the always present and available hostess was posing near the tag-line to add sexiness and style." Scott Makela.

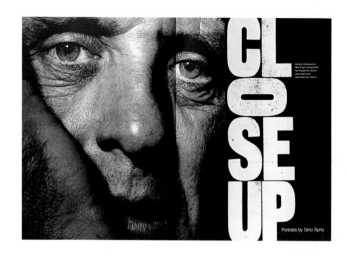

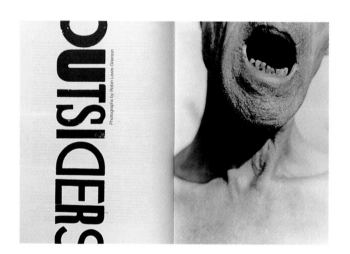

**47** Spreads from BIG magazine featuring wood letter typography. *297mm x 420mm.*

# DELIVERANCE

By Vince Frost Photographed by Giles Revell

**48** CD insert Pay It All Back Vol 4/New Sound Records. *120mm x 120mm.*

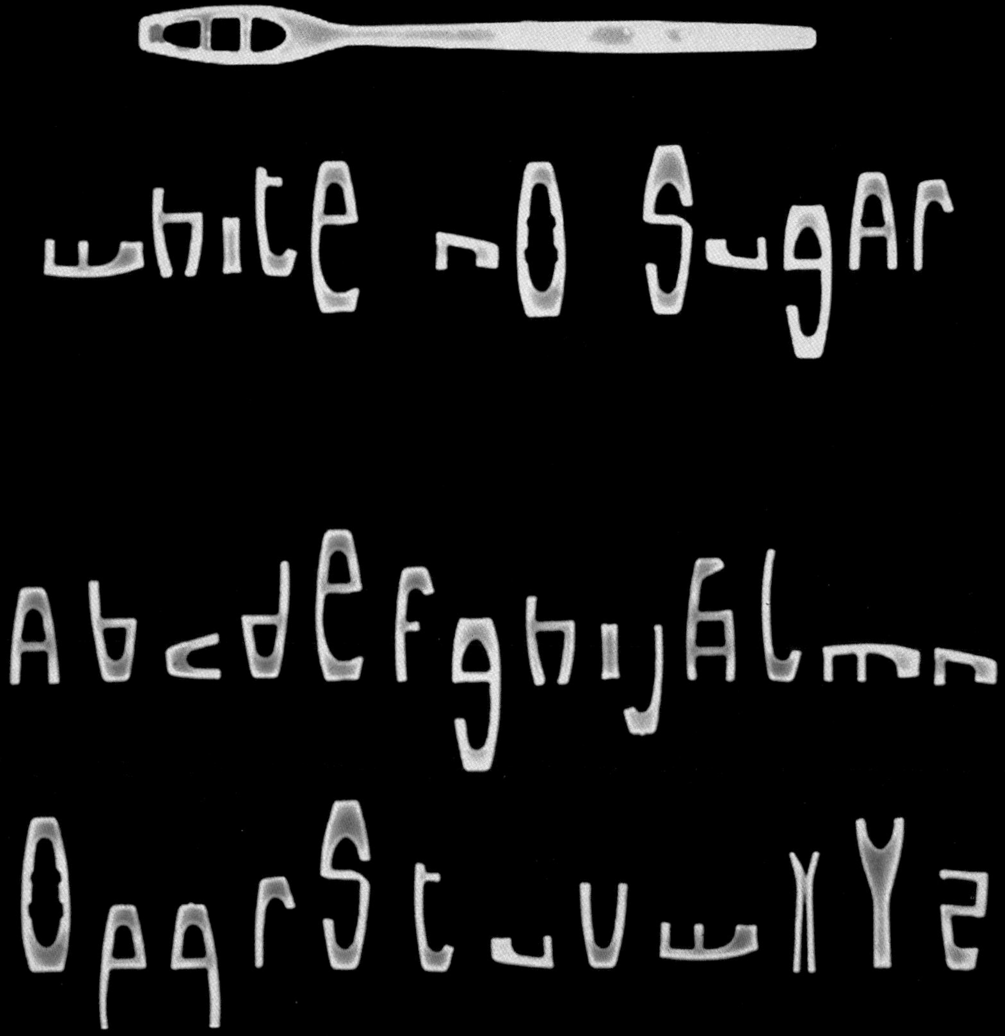

white no sugar

Abcdefghijklmn

OpqrStuvwxyz

**49** White No Sugar, typeface based on tea stirrer.

French Fries

Solitude

A few moments alone

With just me and my bucket of marzipan

run

Continental

new refrigerator full of krispy veggies

ice cubes

Kitchen

telephones

Delicious Fat-Free Snacks

Freon Coils

Potato Salad

**50** Magneto. Font based on the Kelvinator refrigerator sign and old car lettering.

**51** CD cover Brasil. Escola do Jazz/Straight No Chaser. *125mm x 120mm.*

**52** Command Z booklet/fanzine and floppy disc contained in slip jacket. Command Z is a keyboard instruction on the Macintosh computer that restores a previous, erased instruction. *108mm x 152mm x 18mm.*

**53** Cigar band.

**54** T-shirt with logo. *720mm x 990mm.*

# TRUE 10/95.#03

® PUBLISHERS&EDITORS:ClaudeGrunitzky 0171.336.6886/SunitaOlympio.NY.212.353.3867/ARTDIRECTOR:MattRoach@®ASTROSUZUKI:0956.917.907
MUSIC EDITOR:DimitryLéger.NY/FEATURES EDITOR:Ayo/FASHION EDITOR:KarenBinns/FILMEDITOR:AyoRoach.NY/EDITORIAL ASSISTANT:SianJones
FEATURES ASSISTANT:NatashaEggough/FASHIONASSISTANT:ConradJohnson/SUB EDITOR:SimonMcAuslane/PARIS CORRESPONDENT:PierreCortes
ATLANTA CORRESPONDENT:DaraRoach/OFFICE ASSISTANTS:SoniaNimley/DillonVincenti/PRODUCTION MANAGER:FlorenceLartey

ADVERTISING:AndrewBannis/SuzanneAlleyne:0171.336.6886/US.ADVERTISING:JameelHaasanSpencer:212.643.8054
PROMOTION:MoLishomwa/PROMOTION ASSISTANT:StephenMtimkulu/UK&INTERNATIONAL DISTRIBUTION:MMC.01483.211222

WRITERS:CLAIRE COVEY,DARREN CROSDALE,DIDIER MÉDOR EDDIE BRENNAN, ELIOTT WILSON, EMO, FRANK "P-FRANK" WILLIAMS, GREG TATE, JACQUELINE SPRINGER,JOE CASELY HAYFORD,KWELI.I WRIGHT,LISA WILLIAMS,O.J.LIMA,MARCUS BLAKE, MARCUS REEVES, MERLIN MASSARA, MILES MARSHALL LEWIS, NATALIA WILLIAMS, PAUL ABLETT,RAQUEL CEPEDA, ROZANNE WARREN, SABINE BLAIZIN, SCOOP JACKSON SELWYN SEYFU HINDS, THE BLACKSPOT,VALÉRIE BURGHER VINCENT JACKSON, WILL ASHON. *PHOTOGRAPHERS:*ALEXI TAN ANDREW WILLIAMS, AQUILA NATCHI, BARRON CLAIBORNE CHRISTINA CASIANO, DAN WINTERS, EDDIE MONSOON,EDDIE OTCHERE, GAVIN FERNANDEZ, JOAKIM BLOCKSTROM, KATRIN THOMAS, LAURIE LYONS, MARC BAPTISTE, NICOLAS HIDIROGLOU PAUL HAMPARTSOUMIAN, PHIL KNOTT, PIOTR SIKORA,ROB HANN RUVEN AFANADOR, SIMON HORTON, T.MAX. *ILLUSTRATORS:* BRENDAN BACKMANN,GRAHAM ROUNTHWAITE, SENAM OKUDZETO

# FREESTYLE

**55** True magazine. Credits (previous page), contents and fashion story. *228mm x 288mm.*

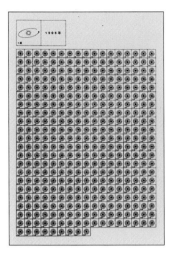 

**56** New Year greeting card.

**57** Postcard designed for infinite flexibility, incorporating astrological indicators.

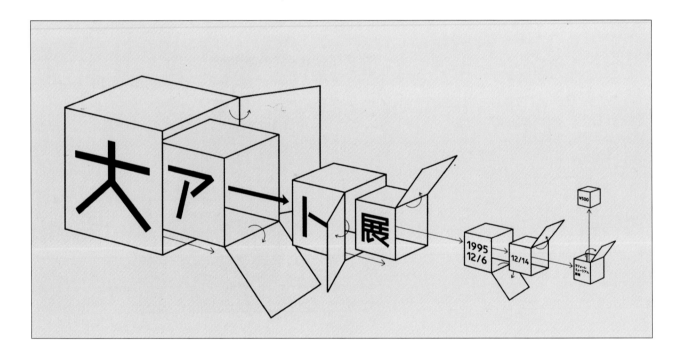

**58** Flyer (above) and poster (opposite page) for Sony Music Entertainment's Big Art Exhibition.

**59** New Year greeting card. Sony Music Entertainment, Japan.

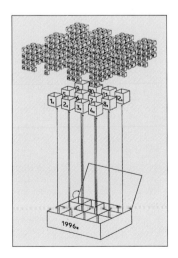

Follow the lines... and enter another dimension

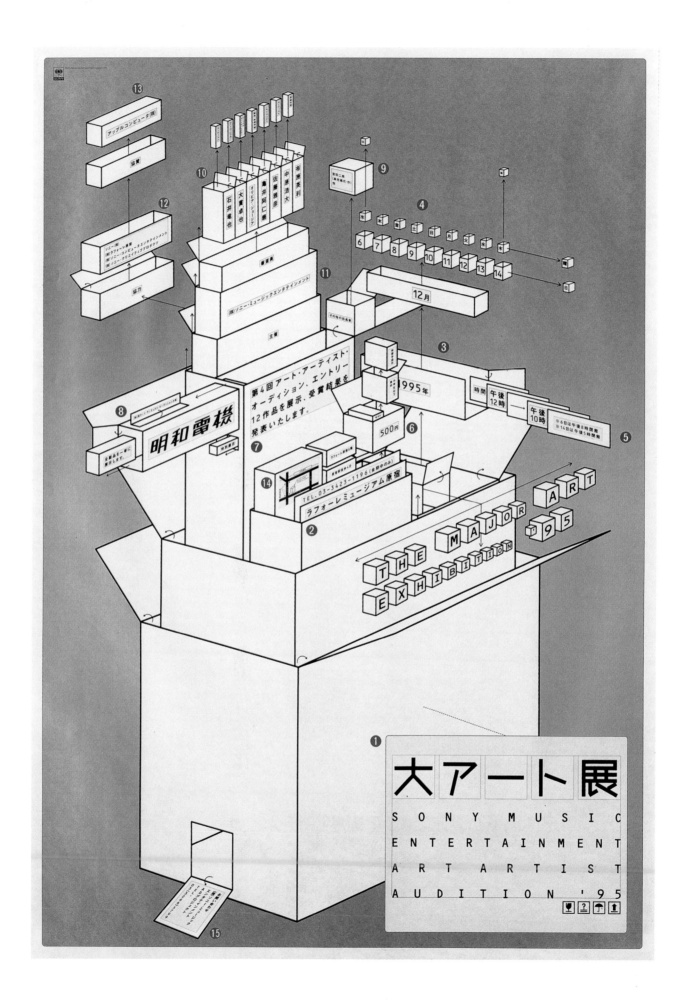

**60** 1959 8mm cine-film packaging.

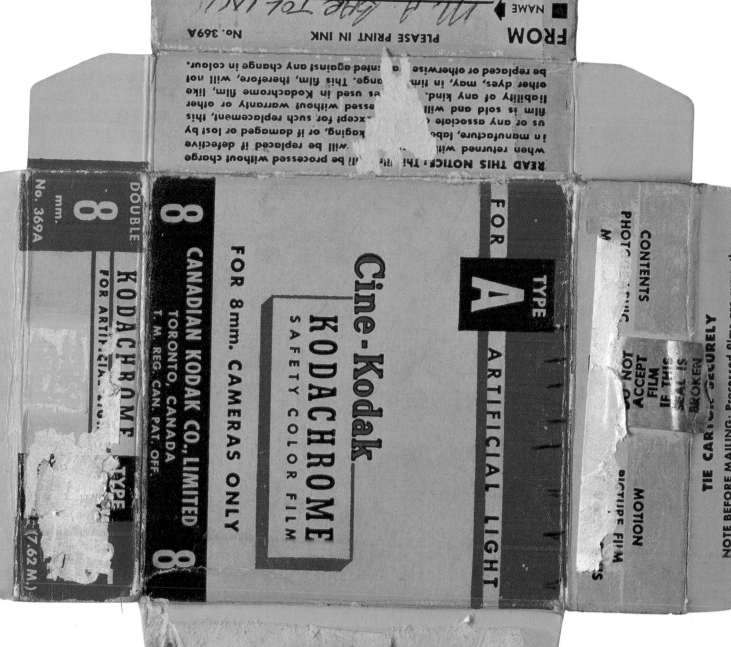

SKATING. - DIANE'S WEDDING.

CONTENTS — SAFETY FILM — NOT DANGEROUS. POSTMASTER: THIS PARCEL MAY BE OPENED FOR POSTAL INSPECTION IF NECESSARY.
FROM
CANADIAN KODAK CO., LIMITED
TORONTO, CANADA
RETURN POSTAGE GUARANTEED

26 II '59

FROM    No. 369A    PLEASE PRINT IN INK

NAME ► M. A. Tolini
STREET ► 930 Burlington St. E
CITY & PROV. ► Hamilton ONT

READ THIS NOTICE: This film will be processed without charge when returned with... will be replaced if defective in manufacture, label... ...kaging, or if damaged or lost by us or any associate c... ...except for such replacement, this film is sold and will... ...ssed without warranty or other liability of any kind... ...as used in Kodachrome film, like other dyes, may, in tim... ...ange, this film, therefore, will not be replaced or otherwise... ...ed against any change in colour.

No. 369A
DOUBLE 8 mm.
8 mm.
KODACHROME
FOR ARTIFICIAL... TYPE
(7.62 M.)

8
CANADIAN KODAK CO., LIMITED
TORONTO, CANADA
T. M. REG. CAN. PAT. OFF.
8

FOR 8mm. CAMERAS ONLY

Cine-Kodak
KODACHROME
SAFETY COLOR FILM

TYPE A

FOR ARTIFICIAL LIGHT

CONTENTS
PHOTO... M

DO NOT ACCEPT FILM IF THIS ...AL IS BROKEN

MOTION PICTURE FILM

TIE CARTON SECURELY

NOTE BEFORE MAILING: Processed films are currently

# 3D

There is a conundrum here. Or perhaps a breakdown in our system. As we said earlier, everything is three-dimensional. Even a sheet of paper has some depth; there is the sense (however unconscious) of two sides and an edge as well as the plane that is being read. Three dimensions seem to be inescapable once we step outside the illusory, virtual space inside our heads. Perhaps you can't even draw that line.

And yet graphic design is typically interpreted as communication in two dimensions. Even when attention is paid to the existence of time, somehow graphic designers and related theorists find it possible to jump from two to four dimensions without recourse to the third. Graphic space-time is a mind-bending world, where two dimensions can be occupied, can be explored, can be comfortable parameters. Accept that analysis, which presents a very flat picture that you cannot touch, if you wish.

However, some messages clearly come with more physical presence than others. Some printed messages play self-consciously with the idea of being three-dimensional (typically by using an unusual paper cut or fold or other treatment). Some stand out for carrying a message on an unusual object – for example, the inflatable postcards or waste-bag poster, included here. Many find ways of using three dimensions to carry messages that go beyond what is possible in two dimensions: the screwed-up curriculum vitae carries its real statement and its impact, its "value", through its boxed, balled-up, unreadable form. But while the printed message may be obscured, many other signals are being sent.

Then there are the many graphic communications that take place in non-print forms – from screen-based presentations in environments, to signage programmes, to graffiti. The methods are constantly expanding, with new technologies and appropriations. Thus the forms of mass, throwaway packaging are transformed into fashion brochures, making substantial three-dimensional statements: would this be anything to do with the fear of being ephemeral, the challenge of making the familiar strange again, of the insubstantial nature of the subject?

This book is also, of course, a series of two-dimensional images that do not reveal all their messages immediately, but have layers of meaning, through interconnections and through the viewer's interaction. The book presents a knowledge of itself as an object. The information is self-consciously explored as a three-dimensional mass, while also playing with time.

This drive for expression-beyond-words is central to the three-dimensional play in design. The vernacular items included here suggest the ways of seeing and the areas that designers are turning to in their search for a new graphic language that lives, that reaches out towards the viewer/reader, that engages by touch as well as by sight. The designer's notebook (pages 110-12) is by its mildly distressed, layered nature expressive of the time and space of the experiences remarked on within the pages. Its mixed media of print, various pens, photographs and ephemera says more about the nature of the object than any literal element on the page or in the "design" of the pages. Of course, it could have been in 4D, or individual pages might have appeared under 2D. We put it here because our interest was chiefly in the graphic object, whereas the owner/creator of the notebook would presumably perceive it as four-dimensional.

Contrary to this are the arresting posters featuring Viking Man and Miss Sissy (pages 108-9). Given our treatment of other single images, these might have been thought destined for the 2D chapter. But the intensity of layers, the need to focus at different "depths" of the images, to journey into the space these create, suggests these posters communicate on a series of planes. Albeit these different levels are represented on the one surface, they require the viewer to refocus, perhaps move closer, to get from the overall image down to the tiny detail of patterned logos, repeated words and the like. Similarly the *Blah Blah Blah* flyposted speech bubble (page 115) is an obvious intrusion on another image, it draws attention to one surface and signals its disruption of that: it puns on its three-dimensional existence and its two-dimensional illusion.

Talking of graphic puns, a popular if low form of visual wit, you might be feeling pretty flat out there. Are you wearing a glazed expression after trying to make sense of this confusion? It's time to give up the debate and get physical, explore the three dimensions. Turn the pages, turn the book, turn the argument upside down.

**61** Rana, a corporate brochure in magazine format, marking 25 years of Frogdesign. A tear-strip at the bottom of the pages removes a section containing potentially inspirational quotes. 80 pages.
*Magazine 229mm x 298mm, strip 229mm x 15mm.*

**62** Record packaging for Dave Clarke Archive 1/
Deconstruction Records. The inner sleeve is
revealed through a cut-away corner, while a
tear-strip permanently opens the sleeve.
*315mm x 315mm.*

**Interaction confers a sense of ownership**

**63** Outer packaging for Images 20/Creative Review Source containing 234 page book (following page). *Packaging 340mm x 310mm x 22mm, book 230mm x 252mm x 15mm.*

**64** Fragment of the shipping box that contained packaged Images 20/Creative Review Source. Corrugated cardboard and tape. *490mm x 375mm.*

PUBLISHER. CREATIVE REVIEW
TITLE: IMAGES 20-THE ILLUSTRATION SOURCE (WITH LETTER)
NO. OF COPIES/CARTON: 18 PCS
CARTON NO. 195
PRINTED IN HONG KONG

**65** Chapter header pages from Images 20/Creative Review Source, illustrating an illustration annual with graphic production artefacts.

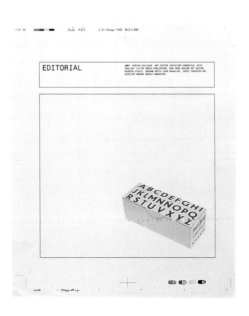

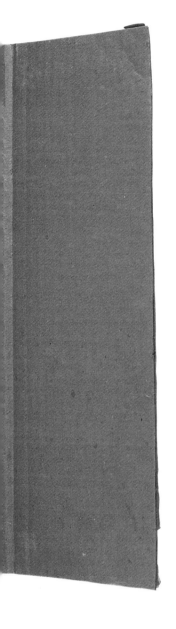

**66** CD sleeves for Massive Attack/
Circa Records. Varied card sleeves,
flat and corrugated. *123mm x 125mm.*

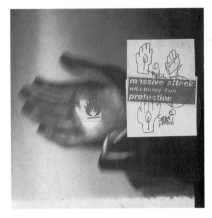

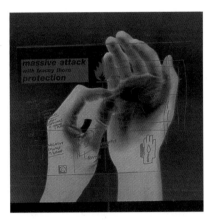

Defamiliarization: the theory that
Art makes the familiar strange

R.NEWBOLD

SPRING SUMMER 1996

GPO

Why is paper square?

**67** Fashion brochure for R. Newbold. Card sleeve containing four circular components. Printed four-colour and silver. *280mm x 270mm.*

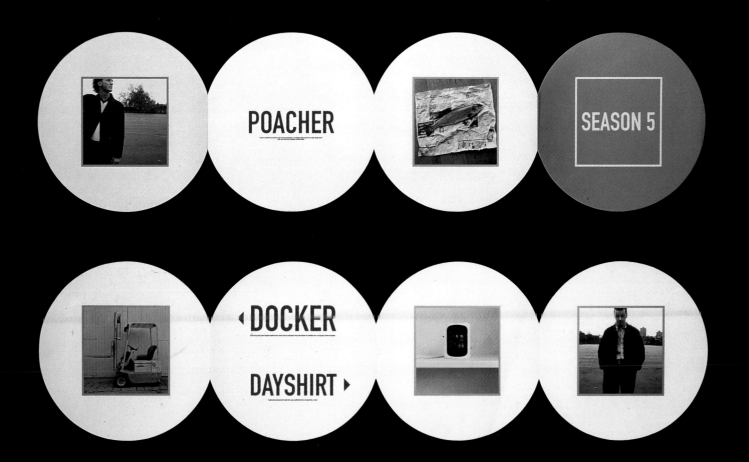

**68** Spread from brochure for Alvin Ailey dance group. Semi-transparent pages with printing are interleaved through the publication.

**69** Polaroid photograph from Jigsaw brochure shoot (opposite page) stuck on paper. *208mm x 297mm.*

Open here

SUSED AS BEFORE
BUT SMALLER
.

**70** Brochure for Jigsaw Menswear. White card with multiple gatefolds that open to reveal the images. *220mm x 147mm.*

**71** Brochure for Zumtobel lighting company. Features die-cut dustjacket that reveals soft cover in fluorescent orange. Pages include die-cuts, with metallic and fluorescent inks. 48 pages. *215mm x 260mm.*

**If white is the presence of total colour...**

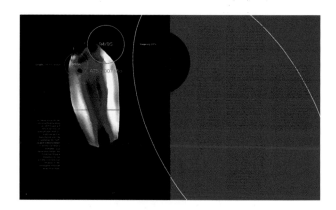

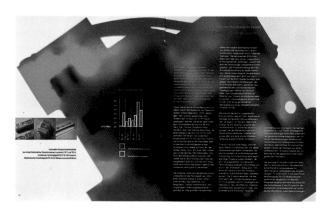

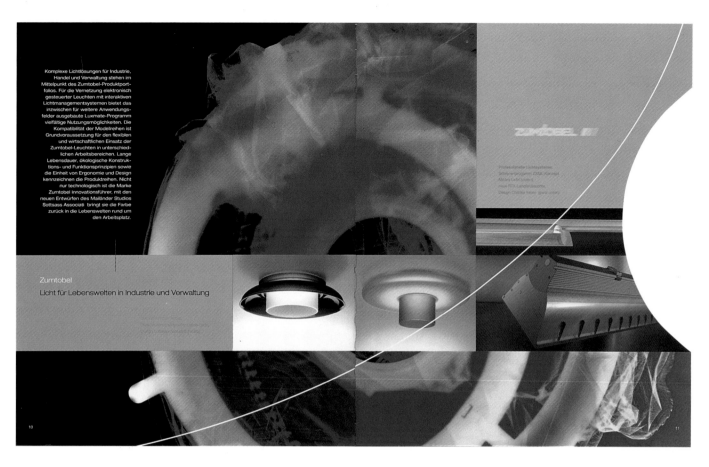

Komplexe Lichtlösungen für Industrie, Handel und Verwaltung stehen im Mittelpunkt des Zumtobel-Produktportfolios. Für die Vernetzung elektronisch gesteuerter Leuchten mit interaktiven Lichtmanagementsystemen bietet das inzwischen für weitere Anwendungsfelder ausgebaute Luxmate-Programm vielfältige Nutzungsmöglichkeiten. Die Kompatibilität der Modellreihen ist Grundvoraussetzung für den flexiblen und wirtschaftlichen Einsatz der Zumtobel-Leuchten in unterschiedlichen Arbeitsbereichen. Lange Lebensdauer, ökologische Konstruktions- und Funktionsprinzipien sowie die Einheit von Ergonomie und Design kennzeichnen die Produktreihen. Nicht nur technologisch ist die Marke Zumtobel Innovationsführer, mit den neuen Entwürfen des Mailänder Studios Sottsass Associati bringt sie die Farbe zurück in die Lebenswelten rund um den Arbeitsplatz.

**Zumtobel**

Licht für Lebenswelten in Industrie und Verwaltung

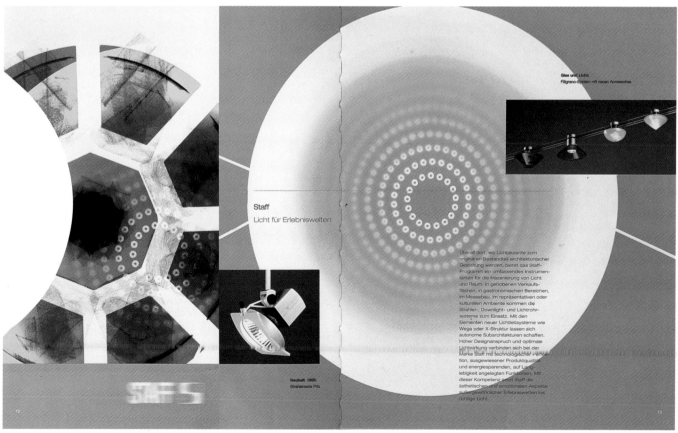

**Staff**

Licht für Erlebniswelten

Überall dort, wo Lichtakzente zum originären Bestandteil architektonischer Gestaltung werden, bietet das Staff-Programm ein umfassendes Instrumentarium für die Inszenierung von Licht und Raum. In gehobenen Verkaufsflächen, in gastronomischen Bereichen, im Messebau, im repräsentativen oder kulturellen Ambiente kommen die Strahler-, Downlight- und Lichtrohrsysteme zum Einsatz. Mit den Elementen neuer Lichtleitsysteme wie Wega oder X-Struktur lassen sich autonome Subarchitekturen schaffen. Hoher Designanspruch und optimale Lichtwirkung verbinden sich bei der Marke Staff mit technologischer Perfektion, ausgewiesener Produktqualität und energiesparender, auf Langlebigkeit angelegten Funktionen. Mit dieser Kompetenz setzt Staff die ästhetischen und emotionalen Aspekte außergewöhnlicher Erlebniswelten ins richtige Licht.

MONEY MARK ⇒

CRY (ALBUM MIX)
CRY (LIVE @ 50 BUCKS)
NEVER STOP (UNRELEASED TRACK)
INVITATION

TRACKS A1 & B2 ARE MIXED BY THE ARTIST
BUSY MARK ALBUM MARKS KEYBOARD REPAIR

ALL SONGS WRITTEN AND PERFORMED BY MARK RAMOS-NISHITA
LICENSED FROM LOVE-KIT RECORDS

WRITE TO MONEY MARK @ :
PO BOX 547
HARDATHA, CA 90248
VISA.

INTERNATIONAL A+R : JAMES LAVELLE.
(& MO BLOND)
SLEEVE DESIGN : BEN DRURY & WILL BANKHEAD.

MO WAX @ED TEL (020)7937 2853 WAX : (020) 735 0645

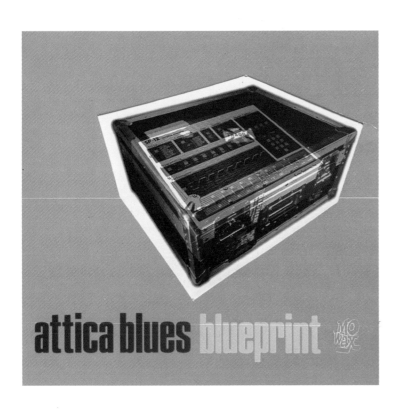

**72** CD covers for Mo' Wax. Card with die-cuts, fluorescent ink, gatefolds. *Various dimensions.*

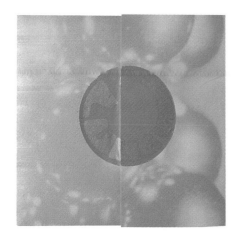

**73** CD packaging for Mesmer Variations/Ash International. Printed cards in transparent PVC wallet. *155mm x 155mm.*

**74** Insert for CD packaging for Wire Behind the Curtain/EMI Records. Folded four times within jewel case. *598mm x 119mm.*

Music: "the combination of sounds with a view to
beauty of form and the expression of thought or feeling."
(From *The Shorter Oxford English Dictionary*.)

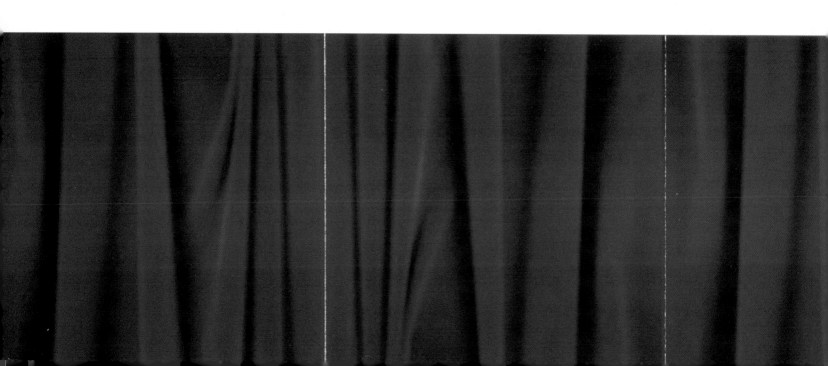

mesmer**variations**

Ash 1.8cd²

7243 8 32403 2 6          WIRE
UK: CDGO 2066             Behind The Curtain

                          EARLY VERSIONS 1977 & 78

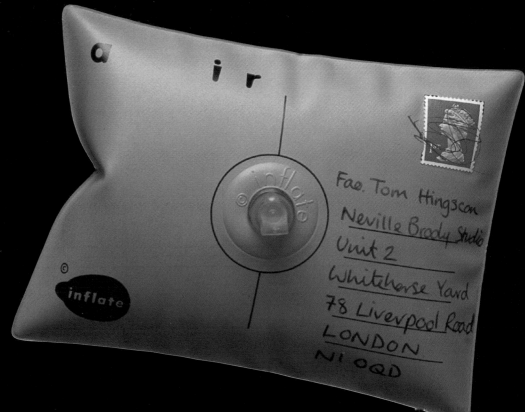

**75** Inflatable postcards.
Yellow obverse, green
reverse and purple
obverse, orange reverse.
Heat-welded PVC with
sealable air valve.
*160mm x 120mm x 90mm*
*(maximum inflated depth).*

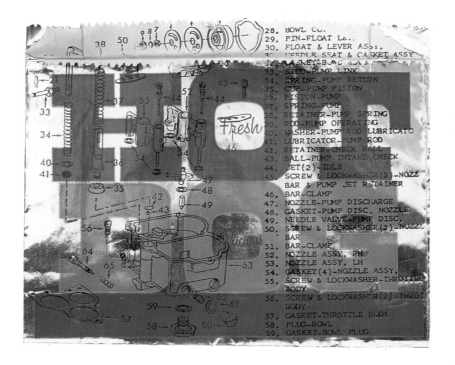

**76** Mailer for artists' agent. Printed paper-backed foil hot dog wrapper. *178mm x 140mm.*

**77** Chopstick wrapper for Oki Nami Japanese restaurant. Unfolded paper printed with origami instructions. Different wrappers for various paper models. *254mm x 102mm.*

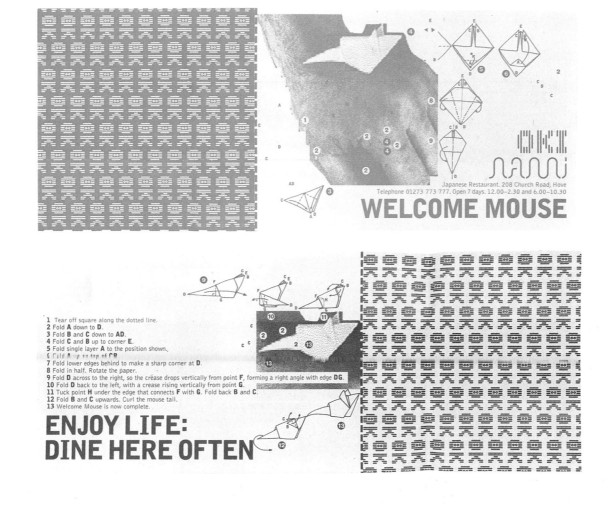

Japanese Restaurant. 208 Church Road, Hove
Telephone 01273 773 777. Open 7 days. 12.00–2.30 and 6.00–10.30

## WELCOME MOUSE

1 Tear off square along the dotted line.
2 Fold **A** down to **D**.
3 Fold **B** and **C** down to **AD**.
4 Fold **C** and **B** up to corner **E**.
5 Fold single layer **A** to the position shown.
6 Fold **A** up to top of **CB**.
7 Fold lower edges behind to make a sharp corner at **D**.
8 Fold in half. Rotate the paper.
9 Fold **D** across to the right, so the crease drops vertically from point **F**, forming a right angle with edge **DG**.
10 Fold **D** back to the left, with a crease rising vertically from point **G**.
11 Tuck point **H** under the edge that connects **F** with **G**. Fold back **B** and **C**.
12 Fold **B** and **C** upwards. Curl the mouse tail.
13 Welcome Mouse is now complete.

## ENJOY LIFE: DINE HERE OFTEN

**78** Fashion brochure for Dolce & Gabbana. Perfect bound, covered front and back with grey foam with printed logo. Contained within blister pack of clear colourless acetate glued to colour-printed board. *Brochure 157mm x 210mm x 45mm, pack 235mm x 380mm x 48mm.*

**79** Fashion brochure for Dolce & Gabbana. Perfect bound in net fruit bag with handle. *275mm x 450mm.*

[Packaging/clothing]

get
Off

WARNING: To avoid danger of suffocation keep this plastic bag away from babies and children.

TARGET FLOOR READY MERCHANDISE PROJECT

OUR OBJECTIVE IS TO RECEIVE 100% FLOOR READY MERCHANDISE BY 2-1-96

Floor Ready" includes the following components:

● Pre-ticketing

● Trash free (no

**81** Fashion brochure for R. Newbold. Grey paper bag with eight 11mm diameter holes. Brochure of 20 pages, with four-colour black and white images and captions, with fluorescent orange headlines. *215mm x 330mm.*

MINER'S PANT

BASED ON THE TROUSERS WORN BY MINERS AT THE TURN OF THE CENTURY. VERY STRONG DOUBLE STITCH CONSTRUCTION. REINFORCED PATCH POCKETS ORIGINALLY MEANT FOR SUPPORTING THE WEIGHT OF PIT TOOLS.

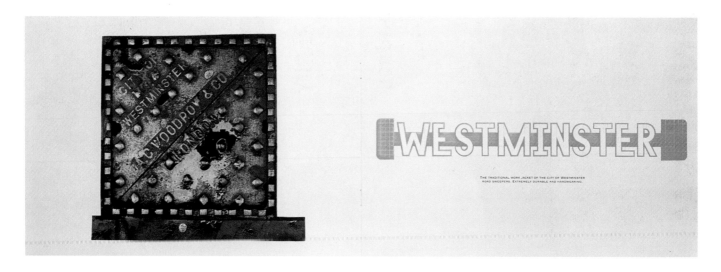

WESTMINSTER

THE TRADITIONAL WORK JACKET OF THE CITY OF WESTMINSTER ROAD SWEEPERS. EXTREMELY DURABLE AND HARDWEARING.

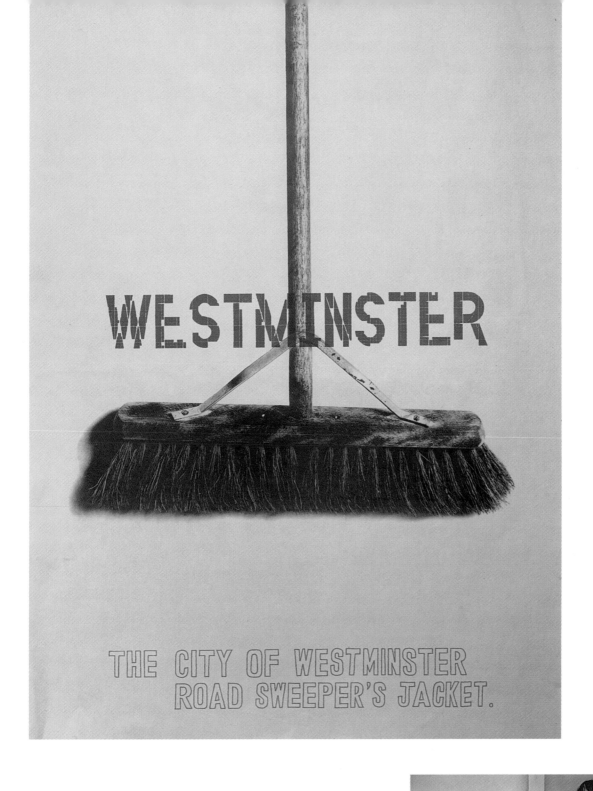

WESTMINSTER

THE CITY OF WESTMINSTER
ROAD SWEEPER'S JACKET.

**82** Fashion brochure for R. Newbold. Newsprint with
random outline and graph paper letterforms. *410mm x 545mm.*

**83** Haemostatic cord. *240mm x 12mm outer diameter.*

**84** Carrier bag for R. Newbold. Logo constructed from holes punched through both sides of a waxed paper bag. *495mm x 485mm.*

**85** Box containing paper samples for the French Paper Co. Blind-embossed corrugated cardboard. *190mm x 120mm x 28mm.*

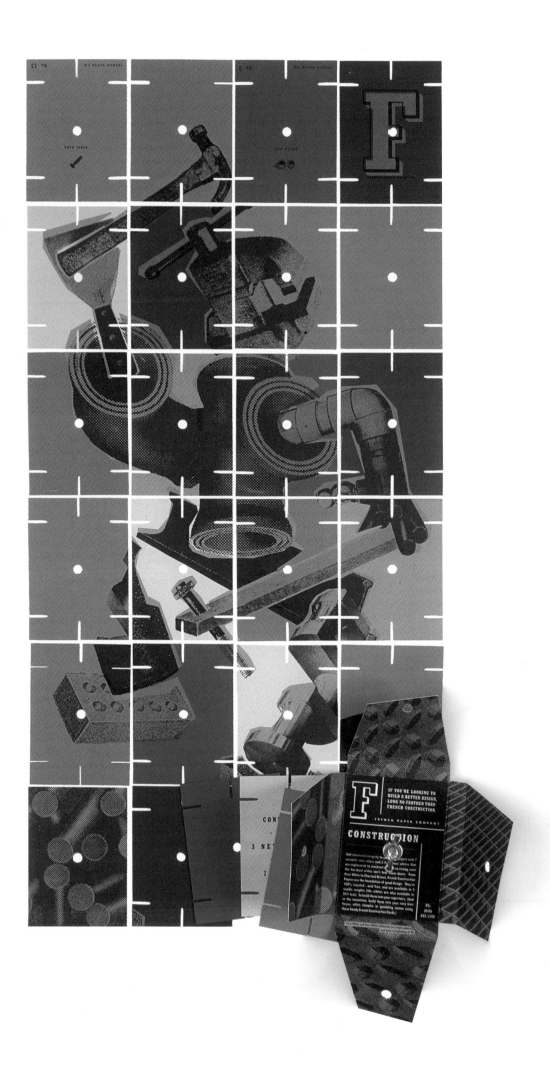

**86** Views of promotional poster/puzzle
for the French Paper Co. Printed card shapes in
card folder, held with wing-nut, can be built into
various forms. Folder *72mm x 100mm x 28mm.*

**87** Promotional T-shirt package for the French Paper Co. Black card box with metal corner reinforcement and adhesive sticker. T-shirt packed under 30 tons of pressure, equivalent to that used in the making of French Paper Co. products. *106mm x 75mm x 52mm.*

**88** Hardback book S,M,L,XL by Rem Koolhaas, Bruce Mau and OMA. 1344 pages. *185mm x 238mm x 72mm.*

**Mass is a graphic statement**

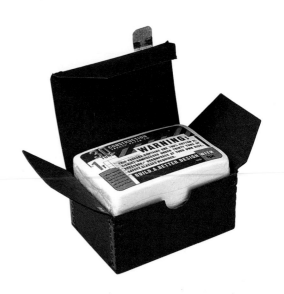

89 Posters. The Designers Republic versus the entire population of Sweden. The Designers Republic versus Emigre. *Both 297mm x 420mm.*

Refocusing on different levels of information delivers an illusion of depth

**90** Pages from diary (here) and
sketchbook (opposite and following pages).
*Diary 148mm x 210mm,
sketchbook 210mm x 297mm.*

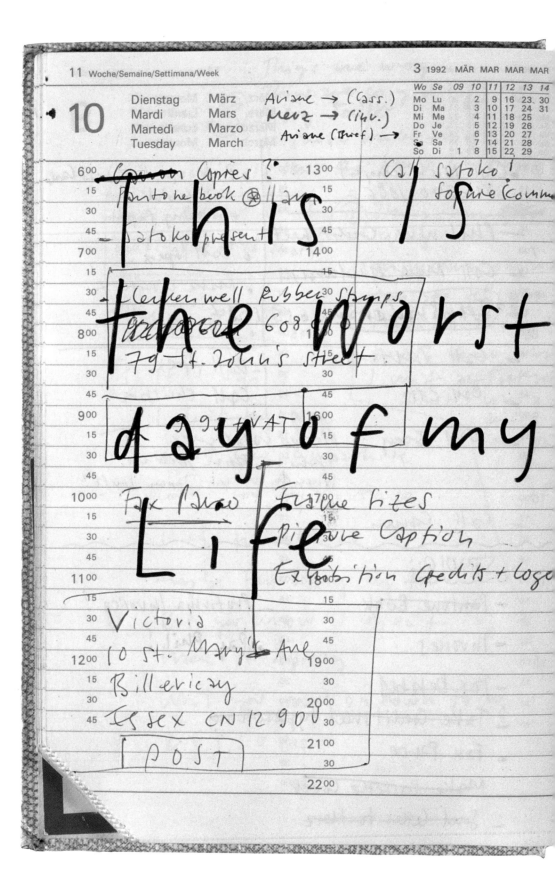

...uuooh!

VICTOR
THE VECTOR
FEELS
WELL

Baby Doll Lounge New York
Baby Doll Saloon Köln

Angela Bulloch – Köln September 1993

GROSSDEMO

"Remembering is a problem"

Globus

Blick
Schock
für alle!

Blick
lügt
wie
gedruckt

Is GOD
in the
house?

Blick
lügt

"sehs.o.mat"

FF Logofonts!

T SHIRTS        Wilson

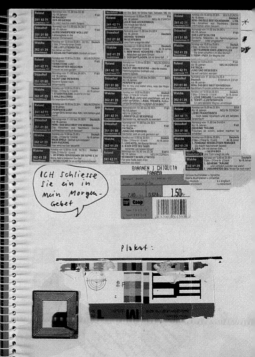

ICH schliesse
sie ein in
mein Morgen-
Gebet

plakat:

*Elect*

Dennis Hopper.

Gurten tragen

... dann bitte ganz rechts

54

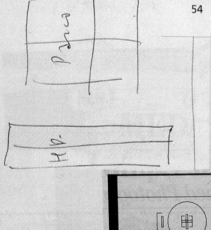

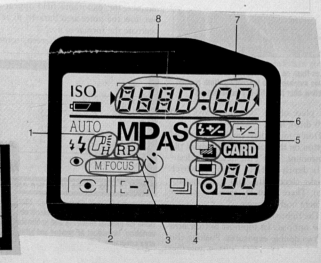

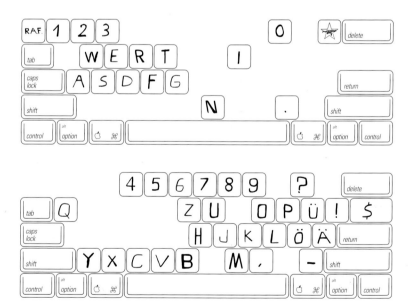

**91** Experimental typeface, completed as F Mogadischu, exploring the theme of violence.

Mogadishu was the airport where a German special branch unit in the 1970s stormed a hijacked aircraft being held by Palestinian terrorists who were demanding the release of Red Army Faction leaders. All the terrorists died, and the following day the RAF leaders were found dead in their cells.

The Red Army Faction then killed a hostage, the businessman H.M. Schleger (shown in picture). The statement in the photograph above translates as "Prisoner of the RAF for 20 days". The typeface is derived from these "letterforms shaped by violence".

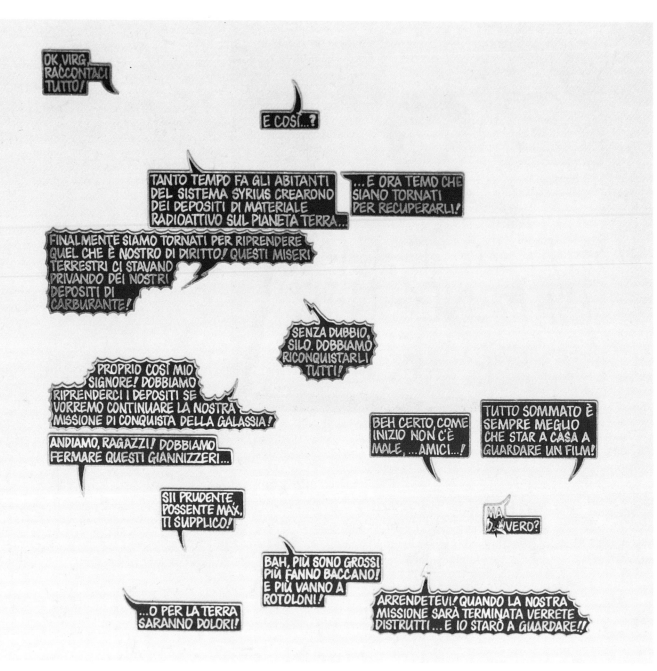

**92** Section of speech caption overlay for Italian comic strip. Printed foil on acetate. *316mm x 187mm.*

**Text is image/image is text**

**93** Flyposted sticker launching Blah Blah Blah magazine by unauthorized appropriation of another poster image.

Graffiti is often a criminal activity, punishable by imprisonment.

94 Three-part poster, a magazine of varied format. Outdoor site. *Each board 1240mm x 2480mm.*

95 Stencil. Hand-cut card with paint. *340mm x 300mm.*

96 Stacked plastic crates.

97 Poster for an exhibition of photographs taken with disposable cameras. Screenprinted black polythene refuse sacks.

"Any graphic designer can appreciate vernacular communication. It is fresh, honest, direct and easy to understand. This is the danger. KEEP OFF THE GRASS." Fuel, 1996.

DESIGNED BY THE PARTNERS  PRINTED BY PURLEY PRESS  CAMERAS DONATED BY KODAK AND FUJI  PLEASE REUSE THIS BAG

27TH JULY-14TH AUGUST AT THE ASSOCIATION GALLERY, THE ASSOCIATION OF PHOTOGRAPHERS

9-10 DOMINGO STREET LONDON EC1Y 0TA TELEPHONE 071-608 1441  ADMISSION FREE

THE COLLECTION IS OPEN MONDAY TO FRIDAY 9.30AM TO 6.00PM SATURDAY 12.00AM TO 4.30PM

# THE THROW
# AWAY SHOW

AN EXHIBITION OF PHOTOGRAPHS USING DISPOSABLE CAMERAS

27TH JULY-14TH AUGUST AT THE ASSOCIATION GALLERY, THE ASSOCIATION OF PHOTOGRAPHERS

9-10 DOMINGO STREET LONDON EC1Y 0TA TELEPHONE 071-608 1441  ADMISSION FREE

THE COLLECTION IS OPEN MONDAY TO FRIDAY 9.30AM TO 6.00PM SATURDAY 12.00AM TO 4.30PM

**98** Curriculum vitae. Sent
as a screwed-up ball, opens
out to reveal black and silver
print on translucent paper.
*594mm x 840mm.*

# 4D

The notion of four-dimensional design is very recent. It took the arrival of new media, notably multimedia as explored in CD-Rom and the internet, to draw attention to the importance of time in graphic design. And yet time is as present in the perception of any graphic design as it is in multimedia – it is just that the new media prompts a re-assessment of what is required, and a reawakening to the issues. That sound, motion, interaction and so on are brought into play in a CD-Rom, does not mean they are less significant in other, more established media. A magazine or a book takes time to explore in any depth, just as a CD-Rom or a net-site does; and such printed artefacts are not necessarily silent, static or without interactive potential.

Not only is multimedia not alone in having four-dimensional graphics, but it also fails to lead our understanding of multi-dimensional graphics. When we came to draw together this section we increasingly found that the new media that had spurred the awareness of four-dimensional design has yet to develop in strictly graphic terms the sophistication and innovation found in older media. For the most part, CD-Roms and internet sites are grappling with the potential of the technology, drawing in ideas from other media. While the sum of the parts is interesting, when the graphics are looked at in isolation they can often be seen as derivative or overwhelmed by the technology. Thus a net-site is typically viewed within the frame of the user's browser software, on a computer screen with the user's system software – and even the page being viewed may be conditioned by default settings within the user's computer. We have suggested a not atypical net surfer's experience of this time (pages 172-3), depicting it as an archival image. Doubtless in a short time the technology will become more transparent, the new content more defined and internet communication will begin to break free of some of the software straitjackets. In the University of Nowhere project, still in its infancy, there is the intimation that things less constrained by the received forms and more driven by new content, are beginning to emerge.

So while we might be grateful to multimedia for spurring the interest in four dimensions, we need perhaps to look elsewhere to find the connections, influences, references that help us understand four-dimensional design. In thinking of the challenge of communicating issues of space-time, it is but a short step to possibly the most influential art movement of the century: Cubism. While there is no immediate visual match between the work in this section and those hugely influential paintings of 1907-11 by Picasso and Braque, there is a strong link when the images are looked at on the conceptual level.

The representation within a single image of several perspectives, of time and movement, plus a break from the conventions of colour and form to a new representation of form in motion, are issues apparent in many of the works in the following pages. In the collages of magazine design – Benetton's image-story Colors issue, or that of the SoHo Journal – in the sharp cuts of film sequences, in the form of a slide show in a Japanese fashion museum, in a photo-essay on Los Angeles… in these projects and more we find designers armed with an understanding of visual language that can be traced back to the Cubist revolution. Inherent in this is a concern for the representation of time passing, and of time as something which may be relative and is bound up with space. Photo-essays and photo-montage most directly suggest this, but so do layered, over-printed texts such as the poem-book included here (pages 155-60).

Of course, to depict the emergence and development of visual form as one based on revolutionary movement, or indeed on revolutionary individuals, is to mislead as much as to inform. There is always a wider context, there are always the wider philosophical and social issues to consider, there is always the change of technology. If there is a key point being made here it is that the concerns of multimedia have been around for a long time – we just have some new tools to use now. As we play with them, so we feed back the context for the next work. This sentence gives rise to the next, for good or bad. Occasionally a word gets to stand OUT. So too, for whatever reasons, a time, an action may become prominent.

When will that moment arrive again? Is the enthusiasm for four-dimensional design a sign that it is now? Time will tell, but we might have something else to do on the day of reckoning.

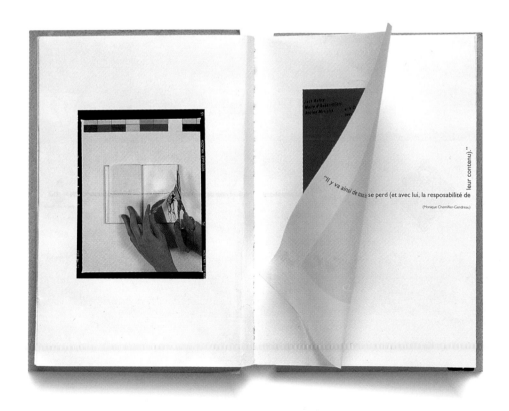

**100** Nous Travaillons Ensemble book of posters with rabbit letterpress on front and sticker on back. Offset lithography inside. Hard covers mounted on perfect-bound soft cover. Images are on outer of bound pages which need to be cut to reveal text. *108mm x 156mm.*

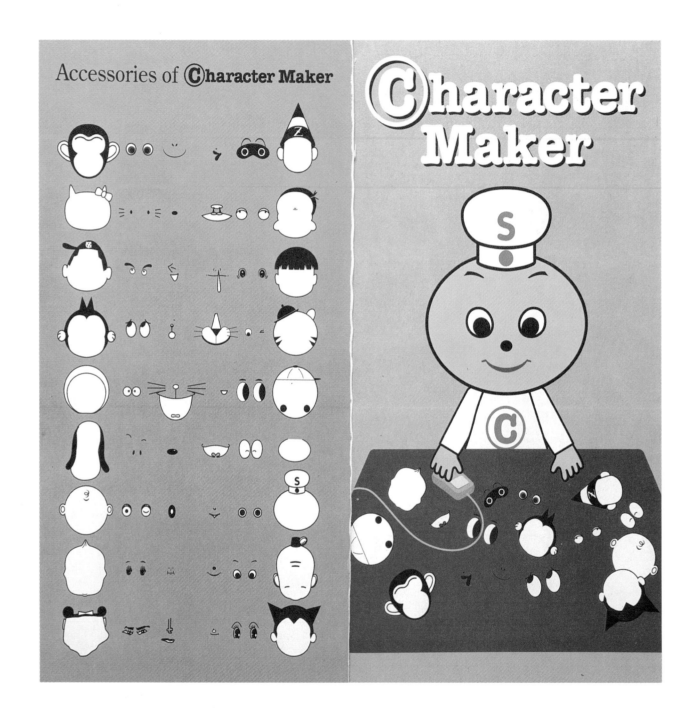

Accessories of Ⓒharacter Maker

Ⓒharacter Maker

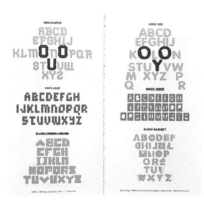

**101** Media of Pop booklet and disk holder packaging and illustrating fonts. Type technology is used to construct characters/images. *140mm x 250mm.*

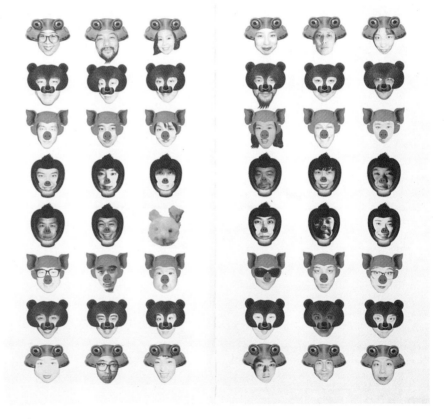

Technologies are being appropriated to manufacture a new visual language.

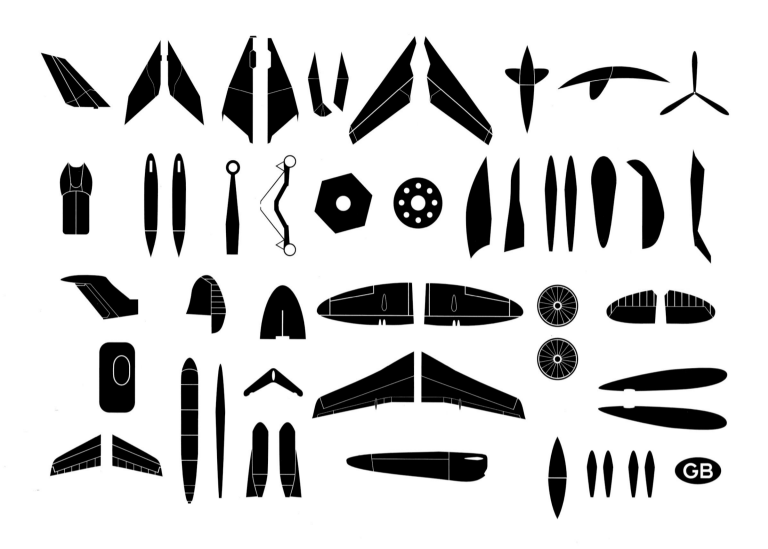

**102** Experimental font, F Terminal 5, provides
the various parts necessary to construct a fleet
of aircraft, stored on the keyboard. In addition,
the upper case characters are connected to a
series of call signs recorded from Russian air
traffic control, and the lower case, a cut-up
version of an in-cabin safety announcement.

**103** Section from model aircraft kit.

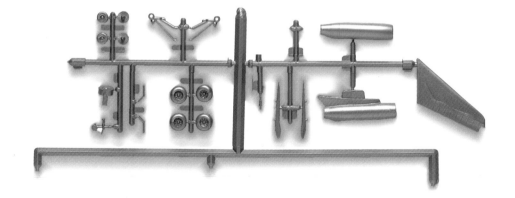

# The future city transcends the city limits. urban roadway takes place indoors the screen. once there, fall quiet, but not only the voice becomes a touch.

© Neville Brody © 1995 FontShop International . Poster printed on recycled paper

FC

the image is the cradle, the eye is now the ear. the action yells onto the screen.

fuse 15 cities features twelve experimental typefaces plus five posters by paul elliman tobias frere-jones lester brunoy and frank heine distributed exclusively through the fontshop network

fuse 15 CITIES cities

**105** F City

**106** F Bits

**107** F DIY

**108** F Determination

**109** F Microphone

**110** Page from Standard Highway Signs manual (opposite). US Department of Transportation Federal Highway Administration, 1979. One of many pages that lays down precise guidelines for interstate road signs. Interstate, a typeface derived from these signs, is used for the text throughout G1.

A = L + 2H + 2F

B = 2H + 2C + D + 3E + 2F + G

H = Border: Signs larger than 10′ x 6′, use 2″ approximately. Signs smaller than 10′ x 6′, use 1¼″. Unusually large signs, use 3″. H should not exceed the stroke width of the major lettering.

J = Corner radii: Approximately ⅛ of lesser dimension (B). J should not exceed 12 inches.

C = Average of the letter height of the adjacent line of letters; C = ½(G + K).

D = Depth of route marker: 24″, 36″ or 48″.

E = Interline spacing: approximately ¾ the average of uppercase letter heights in adjacent lines of letters; E = ¾ $\left(\frac{F+F}{2}\right)$.

F = Height of uppercase letter (refer to Table II-2, MUTCD). Lateral spacing to the vertical

borders is equal to the height of the uppercase letter.

G = Height of numeral (refer to Table II-2, MUTCD).

K = Height of word (refer to Table II-2, MUTCD).

L = Length of "New York City".

1. Calculate total width, A:

"New York City" has the longest length in any line of copy; hence, it determines the width of the guide sign.

Adopt: Upper case—16″ Series E(M) = F
Lower case—12″

Refer to (1977 Metric Edition of the Standard Alphabet Booklet) subsequent pages for tables on letter widths and spacings.

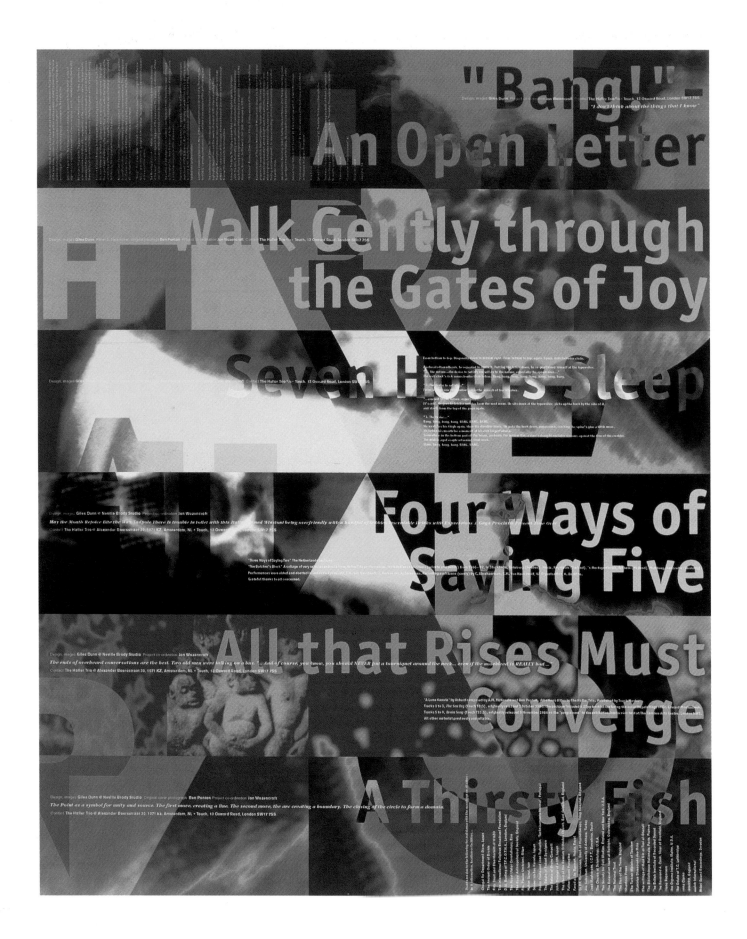

**111** Set of six CD inserts for the Hafler Trio, assembled fronts (above) and backs (opposite page). *595mm x 720mm.*

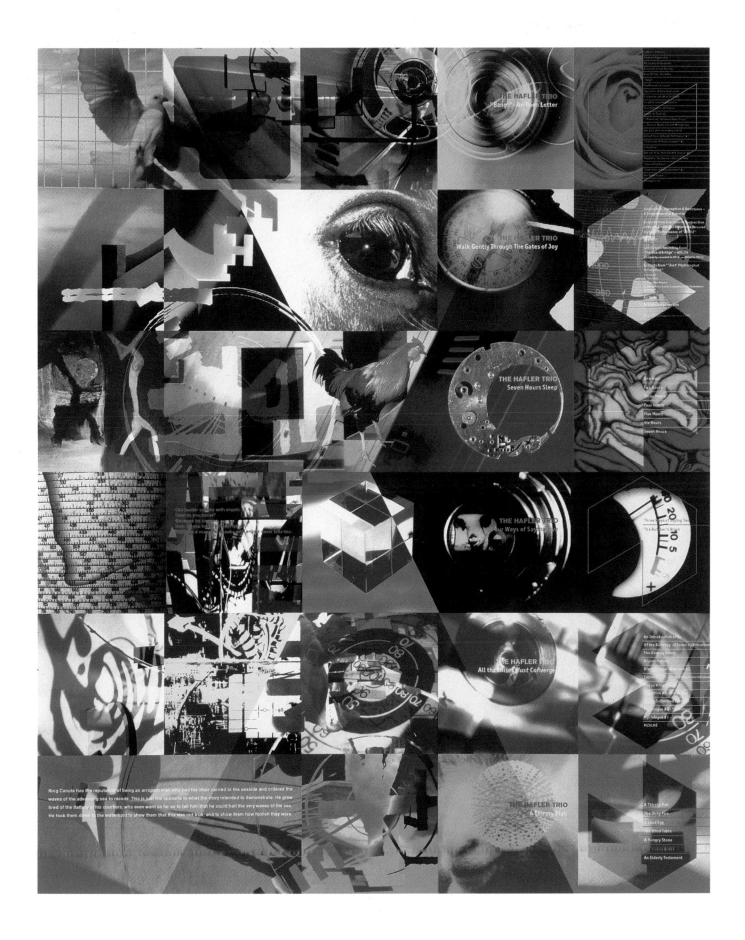

The bigger picture surrounds...

**barbara®**
Tanner Place. 54-58 Tanner Street. London SE1 3PH  t: +44 171 403 3987  f: +44 171 403 1695
design/direction and photography

*I.1*

"the new organisation man is an oral man with a heart of type"

**barbara®**
Tanner Place. 54-58 Tanner Street. London SE1 3PH  t: +44 171 403 3987  f: +44 171 403 1695
design/direction and photography

*I.2*

client list

**barbara®**
Tanner Place. 54-58 Tanner Street. London SE1 3PH  t: +44 171 403 3987  f: +44 171 403 1695
design/direction and photography

*I.3*

projection sequence onto southbank centre
client: THREE'S COMPANY

**barbara®**
Tanner Place. 54-58 Tanner Street. London SE1 3PH  t: +44 171 403 3987  f: +44 171 403 1695
design/direction and photography

*I.4*

extracts from 'BARBARA #1'

**barbara®**
Tanner Place. 54-58 Tanner Street. London SE1 3PH  t: +44 171 403 3987  f: +44 171 403 1695
design/direction and photography

*R.1*

one in a series of illustrations for an article on experimental music.

rd.

**barbara®**
Tanner Place. 54-58 Tanner Street. London SE1 3PH  t: +44 171 403 3987  f: +44 171 403 1695
design/direction and photography

*R.2*

VIDEO GAME packaging for TIME WARNER
client: BEAN Mc

**barbara®**
Tanner Place. 54-58 Tanner Street. London SE1 3PH  t: +44 171 403 3987  f: +44 171 403 1695
design/direction and photography

*R.3*

title sequence: TIME WARNER INTERACTIVE
client: BEAN Mc

**barbara®**
Tanner Place. 54-58 Tanner Street. London SE1 3PH  t: +44 171 403 3987  f: +44 171 403 1695
design/direction and photography

*R.4*

20 second title sequence for channel SC4
client: mustoe merriman herring and levy

**112** Reverse sides of postcards.
The words have the possibility of making
sentences such as "Mum's the word" and
"Fresh salad lettuce", constructions possibly
only available through the receipt of cards
over time. *148mm x 105mm.*

**113** On course betting slip from Gary Wiltshire.
The card number relates to the bookmaker's
ledger entry. The ledger assigns meaning to
the slip. *110mm x 57mm.*

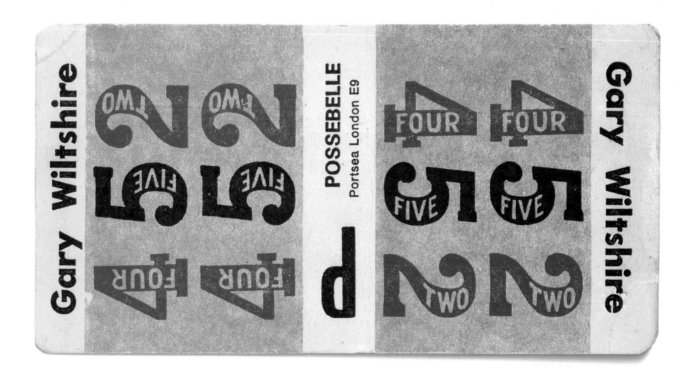

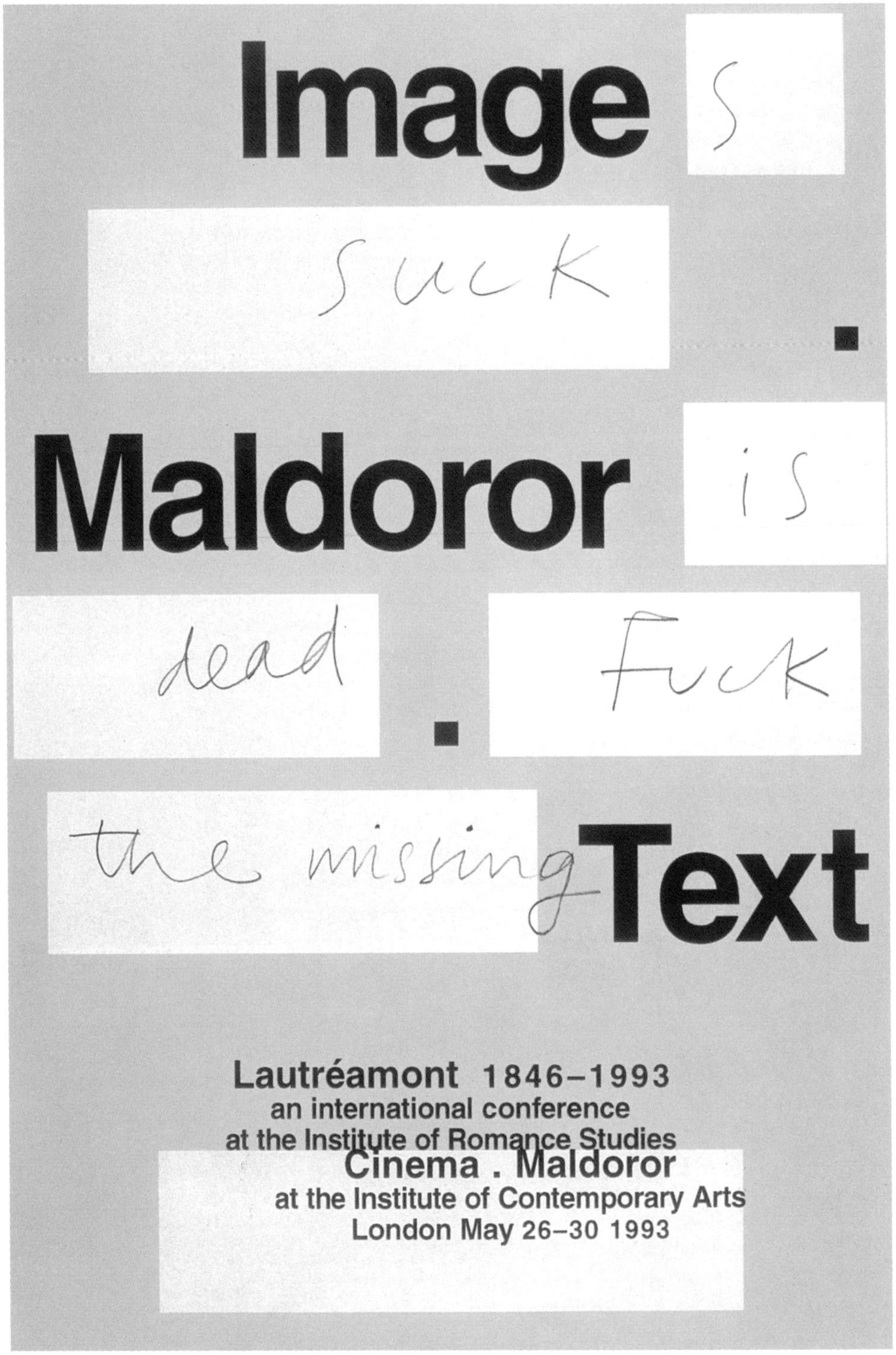

# Image s

## suck .

# Maldoror is

## dead fuck

.

## the missing Text

Lautréamont 1846–1993
an international conference
at the Institute of Romance Studies
Cinema . Maldoror
at the Institute of Contemporary Arts
London May 26–30 1993

Every text conceals or suggests further readings.

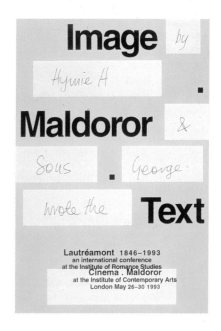

**114** Poster. For conference on the nineteenth-century writer Lautréamont, author of Maldoror. The poster has blank spaces permitting the completion, alteration, disruption or neglect of the message by the viewer. *420mm x 594mm.*

115 Accidental poster collage.

116 Signage for library and poster archive in Chaumont,
eastern France (opposite and following page), using
construction industry graphics and devices.
Environmental signs stencilled on to concrete.
Directional signs on nylon webbing with clasp.
Detail shows sign for silence.

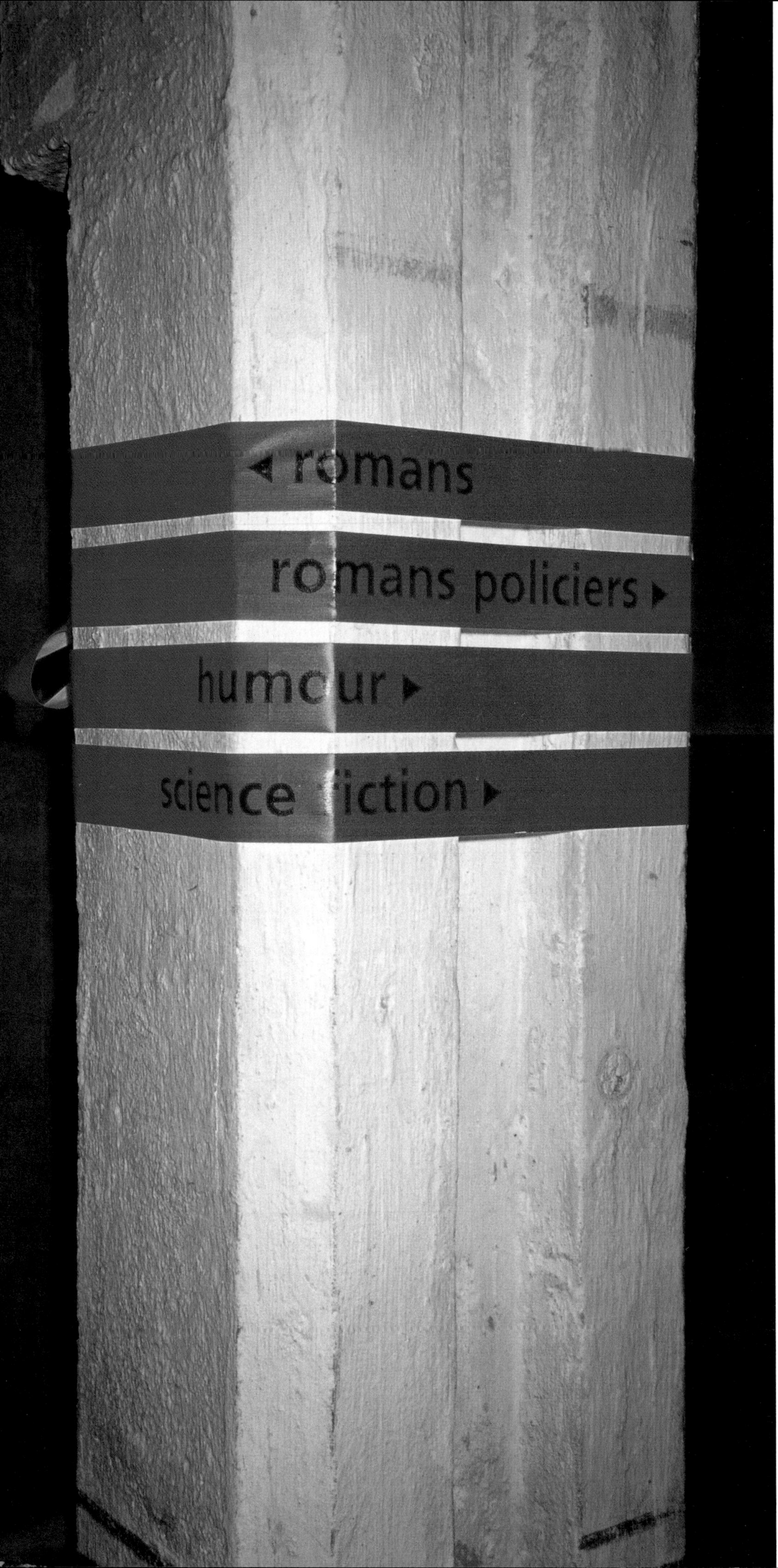

◄ romans

romans policiers ►

humour ►

science fiction ►

現在位置

walls

中学校のグランドの塀

YOU ARE HERE

OMA IN TOKYO 展　屋外インスタレーション

2.vacant lot wall
Torii-zaka(sequential panels)
空地の壁

TN Probe

Roppongi 5 chome Crossing

1.middle school schoolyard walls
Torii-zaka (sequential panels)
中学校のグランドの塀

3.streetside electronic billboard near Roppongi crossing
(20 seconds' animation, per 10 minutes)
街頭の電光掲示板

5.Roppongi station interior advertising poster panel
east exit walkway (poster series)
六本木駅構内の広告掲示板

Roppongi Crossing　　　Roppongi Doori

Boei-cho

Gaien Higashi Doori

4.protective sheet covering construction site
near Nogizaka station (slide projections)
工事中ビル現場の養生シート

Nogizaka St.

TN Probe 34

ロアビルの正面ポスターケース

KOOL

sheet

billboard

都市を謎だらけにする。

工事中ビル現場の養生シート 4

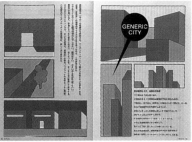

GENERIC CITY

巨大さ（ビッグネス）には理論がない。このことが建築最大の弱点である。最大限、建築には何が可能か？巨大さの理論をもたない建築家たちは「ブラグマティズムの生みの親」といってもいいだろう。建築は部分的には成功したが、全体としては失敗した、という。……「見ると実体の生まれた「同じ」[What you see is what you get.]とは善悪を超えた、道徳とは無縁の領域に突入する。はが大きくなるだけで、サイズが大きくなるのだ。都市……

**117** TN Probe Magazine issue, operating as the catalogue for the Generic City exhibition of Rem Koolhaas/OMA. Architecture/planning issues are explored across photographs of urban spaces and prompt graphic interjections. *183mm x 257mm.*

**118** Greeting card for Cause Première (following four pages), a French organization that raises funds for humanitarian causes. One side takes a folded map of France and replaces locations with words that might be found in a tourist guide. The map reads upside down. The other side takes a map of the Political World and turns the corners into the centre after obliterating the outer reaches, to make a point about the First World's global-centricity.

À peu près joli

Très très

Ce que c'est sympathique !

Quoique

Pourtant

Toujours

Rarement
Rarement plus
Ce que c'est !
Encore moins gentil

Tout
Un peu plus sympathique
Un peu moins sympathique
Certainement joli

Encore plus
Souvent sympathique
Moins gentil
Peut-être joli
Toujours joli
Plus jam

Bien que sympath

Plus souvent sympathique
Joli quoi ?
Le plus joli possible    Quelquefois

Trop
Joli à souhait

Assez ger

Bien sympathique

Tout joli
Joli comment ?
Le moins joli possible

Extrêmement joli

Un peu plus joli
Encore plus joli  Peu gentil
Encore moi
Gentil cependant

Jamais gentil
Fort joli
Comme c'est gentil !
Pourtant gentil

Encore plus gentil
Gentil le plus possible

Joli cependant
Très
Moins joli
Vraiment joli
Si sympathique !
Pourquoi joli ?
Fort gentil

Souvent gentil
À peu près gentil

Beaucoup
Quelquefois sympathique
Gentil le moins possible
Point joli

Ce que c'est gentil !
Peu sympathique
Plus souvent
Pas sympathique
Plus sympathique
Autrement joli
Assez sympathique

Trop gentil
Parfois
Jamais
Parfois sympathique

Où ça gentil ?
Plus joli
Vraiment
Guère gentil
Jamais joli
Aussi sympathique

Un peu plus gentil
Moins joli
Ô combien sympathique  Peut-être
Pourquoi sympathique ?
Tout le temps sympathique
Si gentil !
Moins sympathique
Souvent joli
Parfois gentil
Pas joli
Autrement joli
Aussi joli
Quelquefois gentil

Guère sympathique
Gentil en apparence
Comme c'est joli !   Tout le temps

Encore
En apparence
Extrêmement sympathique
Gentil à souhait

Pourtant joli
Ce que c'est joli !
Encore joi
Quoique joli
Ô combien joli
Apparemment

Pas mal
Plutôt gentil
Davantage sympathique
Davantage
Rarement plus gentil

Quoi ?
Sympathique le plus possible
Plus jamais gentil
Comment ?
Pourquoi pas gentil ?
Bien joli
Peut-être sympathique
Quoique gentil

Bien
Rarement joli
Sympathique le moins possible
Assez
Le moins possible
Autrement sympathique

Quoi ?
Peu
Comme c'est sympathique !
Certainement gentil
À souhait
Très joli
Bien que gentil
Rarement gentil

Vraiment sympathique
Rarement plus joli
Bien gentil
Pas gentil

Apparemment
Si
Plus
Sympathique comment ?
Davantage joli
Où ça sympathique ?
Quoi sympathique ?
Moins gentil
Où ça ?
Plutôt joli
Autrement
Aussi
Autant   Fort sympathique   Point
Moins
Toujours gentil
Plutôt sympathique

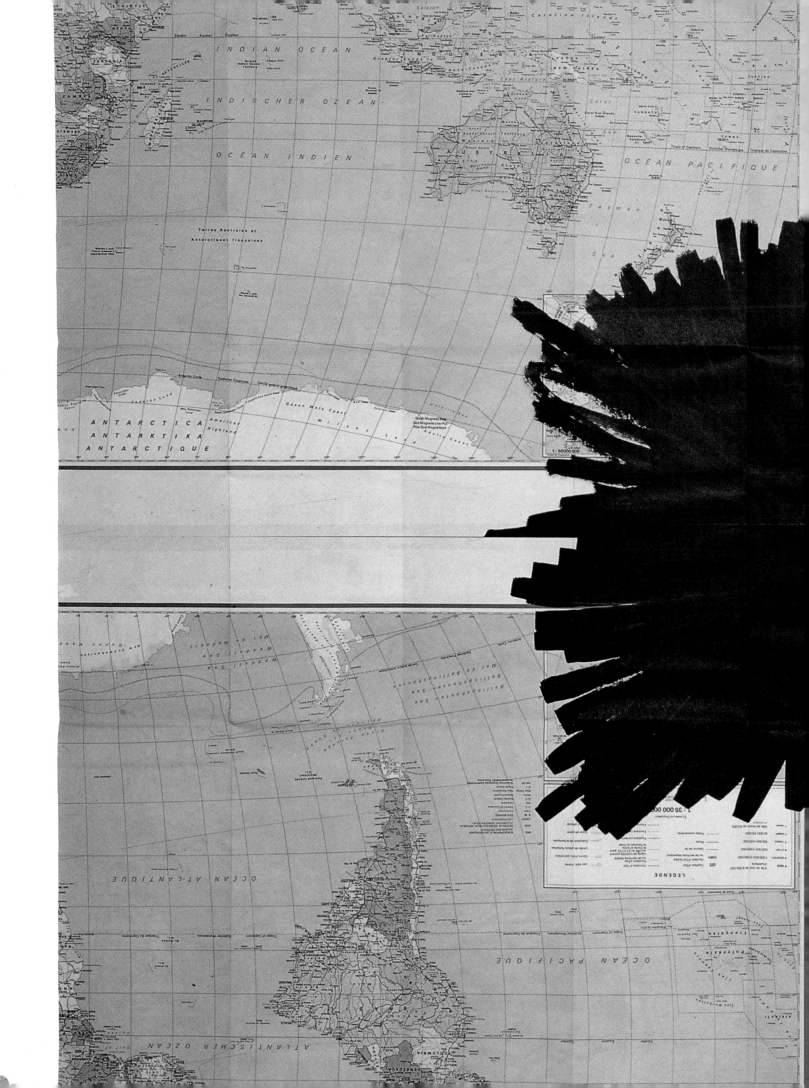

POLITIQUE

LE MONDE

Looking for a City in America: Down These Mean Streets a Man Must Go... An Essay by André Corboz Photographs by Dennis Keeley

Occasional Papers from Los Angeles

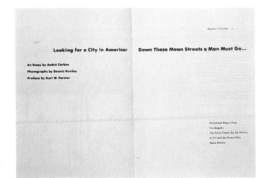

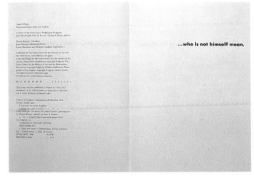

...who is neither tarnished nor afraid.'

"Another author, suffering perhaps from hallucinations, witnessed 'thousands of cars moving at the same speed, in both directions, headlights full on in broad daylight...coming from nowhere, going nowhere.' This amounts to pure semantic uproar,..."

**119** Looking for a City in America... from The Angel's Flight series of occasional papers on Los Angeles, a series named after the black and orange cars on an earlier funicular railway that provided a rare view over the city. The book has an orange cover, with black type. Within is a photographic essay that sandwiches a text-only section. All images bleed. 96 pages. *165mm x 222mm.*

HOMEBOUND
RESOURCES LTD.
AUSTIN, TX 78714-0123

AUSTIN, TEXAS
UNIVERSITY OF TEXAS
CAMPUS - TOWER   25

3 8

HOMEBOUND
RESOURCES LTD.
AUSTIN, TX 78714-0123

3 5

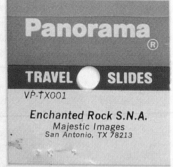

**Panorama** ®

TRAVEL ◯ SLIDES

VP-TX001

*Enchanted Rock S.N.A.*
Majestic Images
San Antonio, TX 78213

ENCHANTED ROCK S.N.A.

TX-ER4/VP-TX001

4. Vernal Pool/Little Rock

ENCHANTED ROCK S.N.A.

TX-ER2/VP-TX001

2. Southern Face

ENCHANTED ROCK S.N.A.

TX-ER18/VP-TX002

3. Vernal Pools

ENCHANTED ROCK S.N.A.

TX-ER20/VP-TX002

5. Enchanted Moon

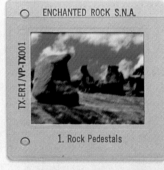

ENCHANTED ROCK S.N.A.

TX-ER1/VP-TX001

1. Rock Pedestals

ENCHANTED ROCK S.N.A.

TX-ER3/VP-TX001

3. Northern Face

ENCHANTED ROCK S.N.A.

TX-ER5/VP-TX001

5. Claret-Cup Cactus

**COLOR SLIDES**

SM-14

**THE ALAMO**
San Antonio, Texas
SCHOOL MART
1812 S. Presa St.
San Antonio, TX 78210

Big Bend Natural History Assn.
#9

Long-spined Pricklypear
and Rio Grande

Big Bend Natural History Assn.
#60

Storm over Chihuahuan Desert

Big Bend Natural History Assn.
#38

Casa Grande and
Window at Dusk

Big Bend Natural History Assn.
#10

Ocotillo in Flower

NO.

DATE

TITLE

Slide•Saver
Made in U.S.A.

VUE-ALL

Big Bend Natural History Assn.
#6

Century Plant in Green Gulch

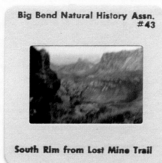

Big Bend Natural History Assn.
#43

South Rim from Lost Mine Trail

NATIONAL PARK

COLOR SLIDES
GM-3
GUADALUPE MOUNTAINS
National Park, Texas

GUADALUPE MOUNTAINS
NATIONAL PARK, TEXAS

Photo: Russ Finley

GM-4

CAVERN SUPPLY CO.

5. El Capitan

GUADALUPE MOUNTAINS
NATIONAL PARK, TEXAS

GM-4  Photo: R

CAVERN SUPPLY CO.

2. Guadalupe Escarpment

GM-3  Photo: Russ Finley

1. Manzanita Spring

GUADALUPE MOUNTAINS
NATIONAL PARK, TEXAS

CAVERN SUPPLY CO.

GUADALUPE MOUNTAINS
NATIONAL PARK, TEXAS

Photo: Russ Finley

GM-3

CAVERN SUPPLY CO.

2. Historic Butterfield
Stage Station

GUADALUPE MOUNTAINS
NATIONAL PARK, TEXAS

Photo: Russ Finley

GM-3

CAVERN SUPPLY CO.

3. Basin Below
Guadalupe Escarpment

SARBO-SEENS
by SARBO®

BOX.5171
ALBUQUERQUE, N.M. 87185

IN POPULAR 35MM SIZE
TO MATCH YOUR OWN

NORTHERN
NEW MEXICO          NO-1

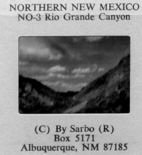

NORTHERN NEW MEXICO
NO-3 Rio Grande Canyon

(C) By Sarbo (R)
Box 5171
Albuquerque, NM 87185

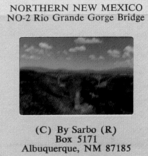

NORTHERN NEW MEXICO
NO-2 Rio Grande Gorge Bridge

(C) By Sarbo (R)
Box 5171
Albuquerque, NM 87185

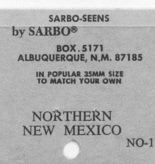

NORTHERN NEW MEXICO
NO-5 Palisades - Cimarron Canyon

(C) By Sarbo (R)
Box 5171
Albuquerque, NM 87185

NORTHERN NEW MEXICO
NO-4 Sangre de Cristo Mts
& Arroyo Hondo Village

(C) By Sarbo (R)
Box 5171
Albuquerque, NM 87185

INDIAN PETROGLYPHS
IP-1  Spiral and Sun Symbol

© By Sarbo ®
Box 5171
Albuquerque, NM 87185

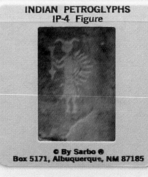

INDIAN PETROGLYPHS
IP-4  Figure

© By Sarbo ®
Box 5171, Albuquerque, NM 87185

SARBO-SEENS
by SARBO®

BOX 5171
ALBUQUERQUE, N.M. 87185

IN POPULAR 35MM SIZE
TO MATCH YOUR OWN

TAOS, N.M.          TS-2

TAOS, N.M.
TS-23  Close-up - North Pueblo

© By Sarbo ®
Box 5171
Albuquerque, NM 87185

TAOS, N.M.
TS-21  North Pueblo

© By Sarbo ®
Box 5171
Albuquerque, NM 87185

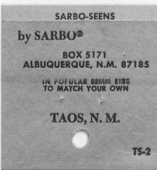

**120** Various packs of souvenir 35mm slides, collected on a journey from Austin, Texas to Albuquerque, New Mexico.

```
        SOMERFIELD STORES LIMITED
      WHITCHURCH BRISTOL BS14 OTJ
                BARKING
         VAT NO. 107 4212 12
           0181 591 9363

                               £
         MIX PEPPERS        1.29
   NEW POTATOES
     1.12 lb @   £0.32/lb   0.36
        ORANGES LGE         0.79
   BANANAS
     1.63 lb @   £0.35/lb   0.57
     GRANNY SMITHS
     2.32 lb @   £0.38/lb   0.88
   ONIONS
     1.42 lb @   £0.16/lb   0.23
     CARROTS
     1.04 lb @   £0.16/lb   0.17
     TOMATOES
     2.50 lb @   £0.89/lb   2.23
   MUSHROOMS
     0.54 lb @   £1.59/lb   0.86
     COURGETTES
     0.47 lb @   £1.19/lb   0.56
     SWEDE
     1.88 lb @   £0.22/lb   0.41
        SHAMPOO             0.99
        KITCHEN FOIL        0.83
        FELIX               0.45
        SPAGHETTI           0.13
        BAKED BEANS         0.12
        BAKED BEANS         0.12
        FELIX TUNA          0.45
        FELIX               0.45
        FELIX               0.45
        BAKED BEANS         0.12
        FELIX TRT/SH        0.45
        FELIX TRT/SH        0.45
        FELIX LB/HRT        0.45
        BAKED BEANS         0.12
        BAKED BEANS         0.12
        RED KID BEAN        0.25
        SWEETCORN           0.39
        SWEETCORN           0.39
        SWEETCORN           0.39
        SWEETCORN           0.39
        RED KID BEAN        0.25
        SWEETCORN           0.39
        SF BASIC S/F        0.24
        RED KID BEAN        0.25
        RED KID BEAN        0.25
        MILD CHEDDAR        3.09
        SF C/FLAKES         0.55
        SOY SAUCE           0.56
        BASIC BREAD         0.27
     SF COTT CHSE
        REDUCED PRICE       0.30
        GROCERY             0.25
        HALF FAT            1.33
        ORANGE JUICE        0.48
        ORANGE JUICE        0.48
        ORANGE JUICE
        REDUCED PRICE       0.40
        AQUA PURA           0.62
        SF SGLEN SPK        0.75

     48 BAL DUE            26.32

   EFT                     26.32
   3   675960 01379 6867 2567
   CHANGE                   0.00

   2170 13  54 7088 17:46  4JAN96

        SAVINGS THAT
            ADD UP
```

Even tea towels write letters

**121** Map of shopping route. By handing items to the cashier in the same order as they were picked from the shelves, a route around the supermarket has been documented. *76mm x 324mm.*

**122** Non-commissioned photograph presenting a tea-towel holder as a family of xs. Degrees of wear provide different weights.

**123** Fashion brochure for Diesel (here and following pages) explores "myths and fears" of modern living. The fashion victim suffers across a wider front than clothing, in stories that play on the confessional magazine genre. Perfect bound in uncoated card. *230mm x 295mm.*

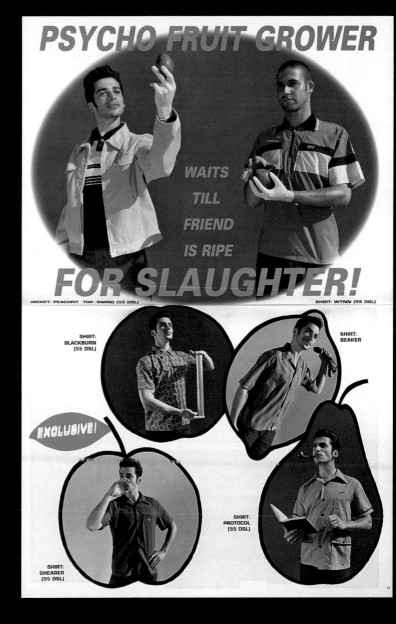

How we read. How we think.

## BASIC PRINCIPLES

# TERMINOLOGY OF SKIN LESIONS

The words used in dermatology vary from those used in other medical disciplines and are an essential part of the process of accurately describing acute skin disorders. For instance, LESIONS may refer to <u>small</u> areas of infected tissue. ERUPTION (or RASH) would describe more succulent and widespread conditions.

## MACULE

Areas of the skin are subject to sudden COLOUR CHANGE. This will however leave the quality of the skin surface unaltered. As is already well-known, macules are sometimes hypopigmented. The common freckle is a <u>pigmented</u> example.

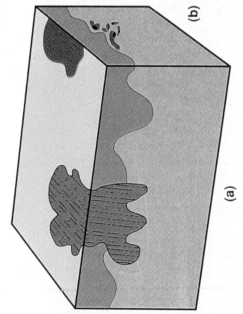

(a)

(b)

## BULLA

These are NOT to be confused with VESICLES (smaller than 5mm) Good examples of this condition are <u>blisters</u> (pemphigus vulgaris and bullous pemphigoid).

**DANGER**

Fig.1   Jacket: Lap

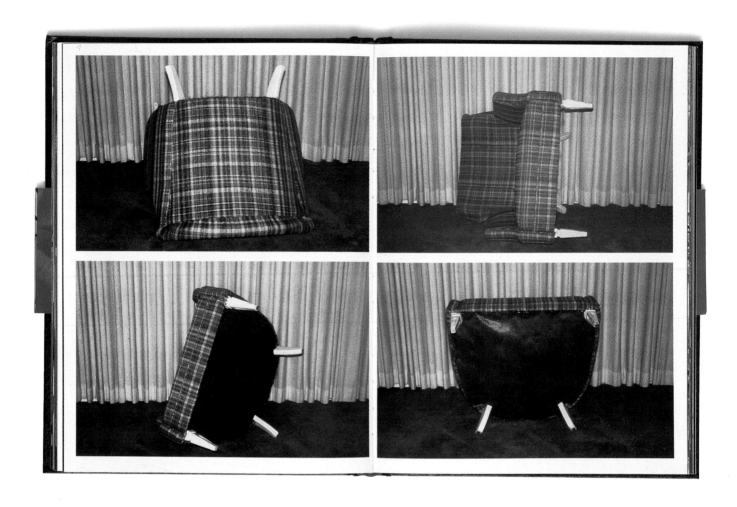

**I WORSHIP THESE**

I worship fame. I worship what I don't understand. I worship beauty. I worship bargains.
I worship heavily spiced foods. I worship community. I worship primary colors.
I worship obsessive behavior in others. I worship meaningless images.

**124** Strange Ritual (here and previous pages), a book of images by David Byrne. 174 pages. *195mm x 261mm.*

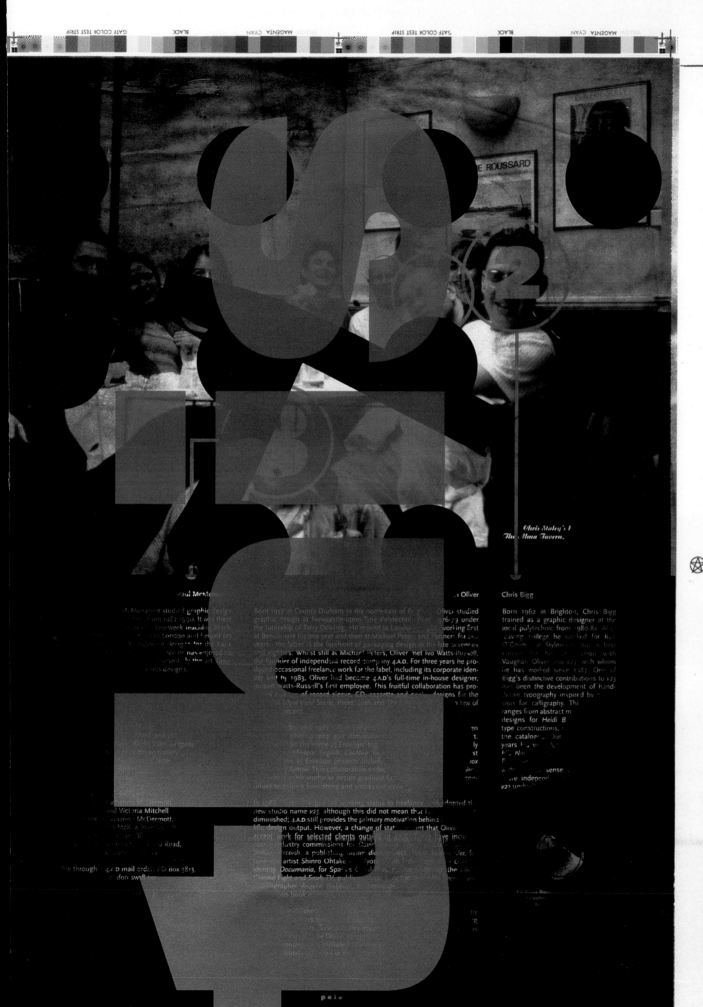

Chris Staley's t
The Alma Tavern,

**Paul McMena**

Mc Menamin studied graphic design
from 1987-1990. It was there
... two-week teaching block
... to London and helped est
... include designs for the Paris
... he has enjoyed an
... currently the art di...
... ions designs;

Born 1957 in County Durham in the north-east of E... Oliver studied
graphic design at Newcastle-upon-Tyne Polytechnic from 1976-79 under
the tutorship of Terry Dowling. He moved to Londo... working first
at Benchmark for one year and then at Michael Peters and Partners for two
years—the latter at the forefront of packaging design in the late seventies
and eighties. Whilst still at Michael Peters, Oliver met Ivo Watts-Russell,
the founder of independent record company 4.A.D. For three years he produced occasional freelance work for the label, including its corporate identity and by 1983, Oliver had become 4.A.D's full-time in-house designer,
... Watts-Russell's first employee. This fruitful collaboration has produced ... of record-sleeve, CD, cassette-and-poster designs for the
... Ultra Vivid Scene, Pixies, Lush and the ... n few of
... ...

**Chris Bigg**

Born 1962 in Brighton, Chris Bigg
trained as a graphic designer at the
local polytechnic from 1980-83. Af...
leaving college he worked for Ro...
O'Connor at Stylorou... but is best
known for his ... ation with
Vaughan Oliver and v23 with whom
he has worked since 1987. One of
Bigg's distinctive contributions to v23
has been the development of hand-
drawn typography inspired by ...
... sion for calligraphy. Thi...
ranges from abstract m...
designs for Heidi B...
type constructions, ...
the catalogu... Dur...
years he w... for...
H. Nai...
B...
w... ... sense ...
... ...e independen...
v23 umbrel...

and Victoria Mitchell
...ith ... McDermott,
... McKe...
... ...d Road,
...
... through 4.A.D mail order, PO Box 3813,
... don sw18 ...

... to freela... ...dopted th...
new studio name v23 although this did not mean that ...
diminished; 4.A.D still provides the primary motivation behind ...
...lific design output. However, a change of stat... ...nt that Olive...
accept work for selected clients outsi... ... ...ve inclu...
... dustry commissions for Davi...
... ecords, a publishing ...eam dic... ...ject ... Schnei der, for
Japan... artist Shinro Ohtake ... Kyoto ... in Feb... ... id...
identity, Documania, for Spai...s C... ...bras, ...mme... ... the ...
Gimme Eight and Snub TV, a publi... design direc for ... ...phen... and
... ...grapher Angelin... Wai...co ...m...
... his book ...

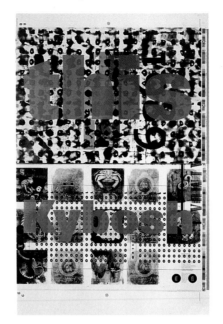

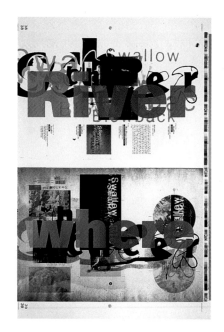

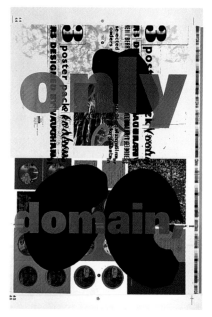

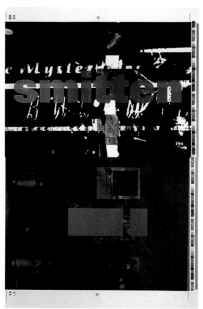

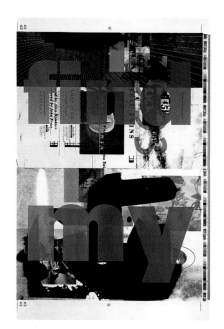

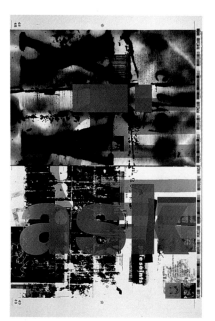

158

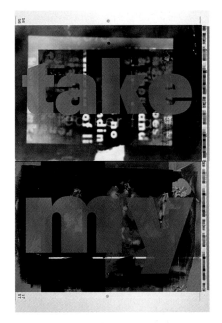

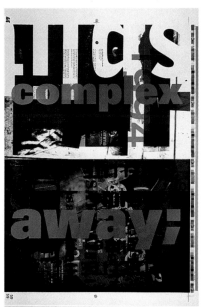

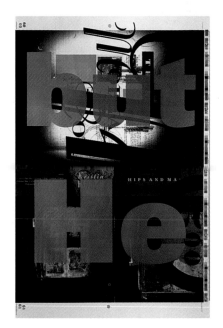

**125** Book formed by over-printing sheets left over from an exhibition catalogue of designer's own work (pages 155-60). The poem "This Rimy River" is over-printed in black and gold. The page size is trimmed larger than the original catalogue. *270mm x 375mm.*

this Fabled Fracas is impenetrable
could kick this Kybosh to Kingdom Come –
Dote and Passion need the wallow of warmth
am I so inca-ca-capable? Christ!
weirdos, Bedlam, blitz below
begone and scam!
drift and drain this Rimy River
where smitten I find my only domain,
engrossed, ensnarled I ask The Boatswain
for His pipe to take my complex away;
but He say:
exposed is exposed there is no more danger than that.

⑤ ART

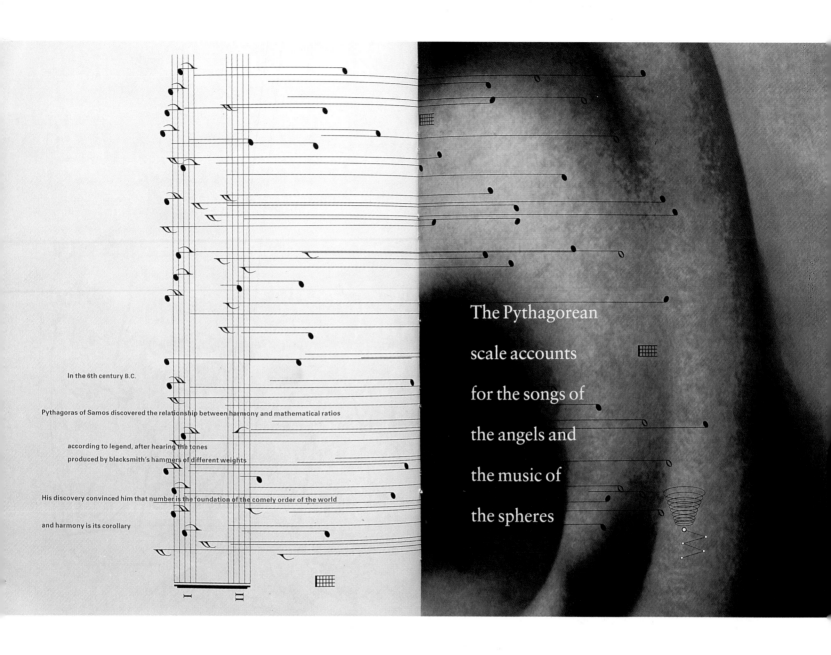

In the 6th century B.C.

Pythagoras of Samos discovered the relationship between harmony and mathematical ratios

according to legend, after hearing the tones
produced by blacksmith's hammers of different weights

His discovery convinced him that number is the foundation of the comely order of the world

and harmony is its corollary

The Pythagorean

scale accounts

for the songs of

the angels and

the music of

the spheres

What is used as an element in a machine          is in fact an element in the machine

The aggressive stylization of this mass-produced cockpit, the exaggerated mouldings of the instrument binnacles emphasized my growing sense of a new junction between my own body and the automobile, closer than my feelings for Renata's broad hips and strong legs stowed out of sight beneath her red plastic raincoat. I leaned forward, feeling the rim of the steering wheel against the scars on my chest, pressing my knees against the ignition switch and handbrake

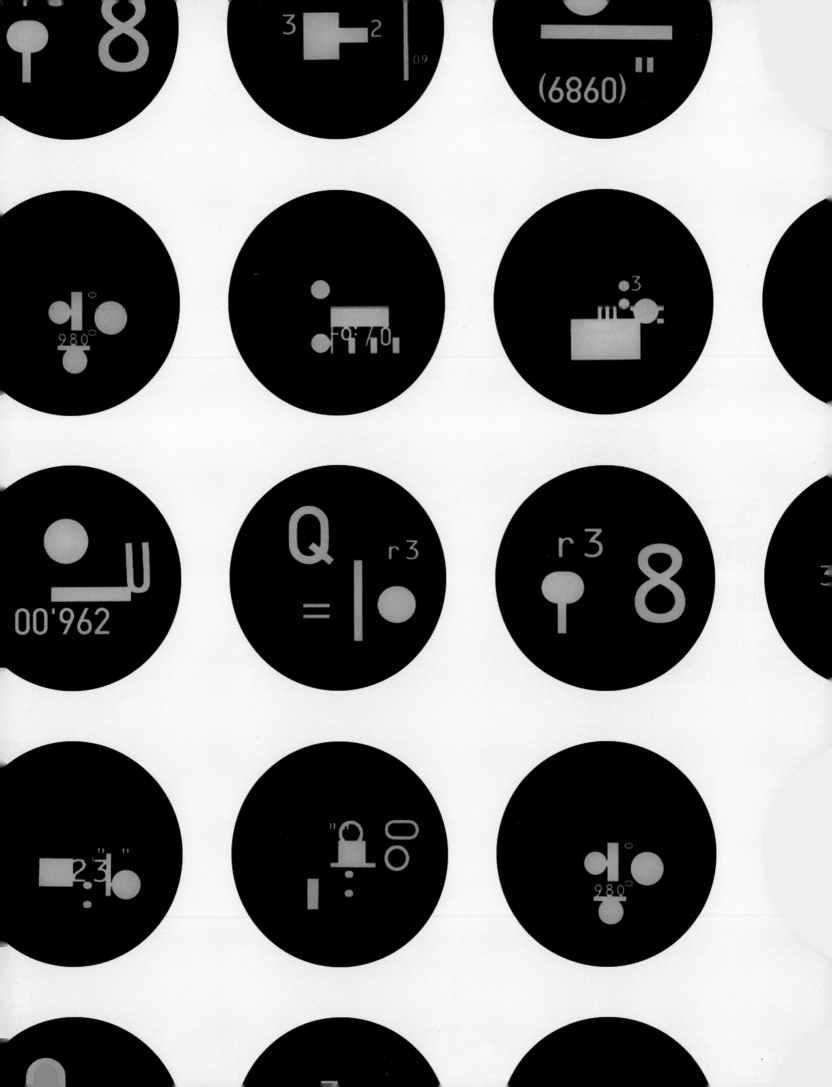

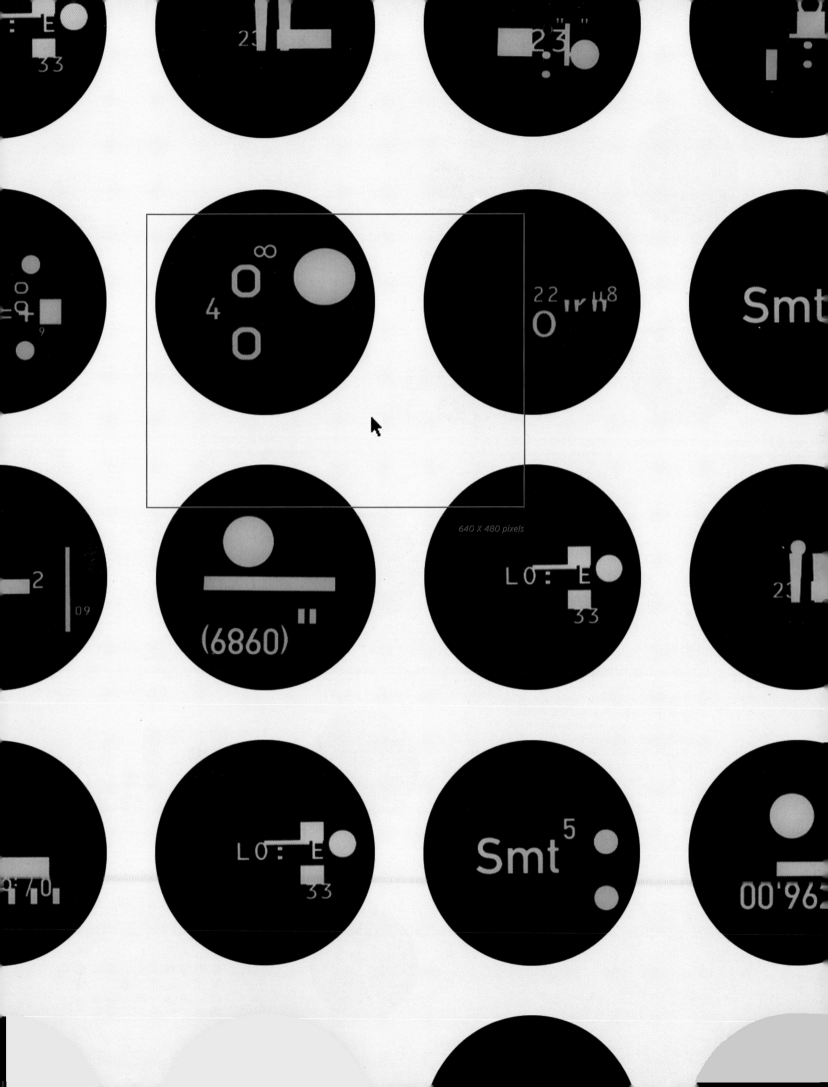

640 X 480 pixels

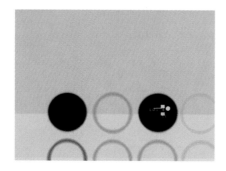

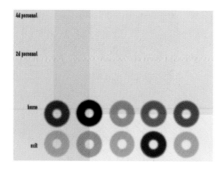

**127** Extract from CD-Rom, A Tomato Project
(here and previous pages), a showcase and
re-editing of design and film work. As the cursor
moves over the circles, different music tracks
come into play; click on the circles to enter different
sections of the disk. Most of the sound and image
is abstract, in that it is without precise boundaries
or reference. Once finite graphic works are re-edited
to become indeterminate. The previous pages show
the underlying grid of circles from which only a few
are visible at any one time to the viewer moving
around the screen.

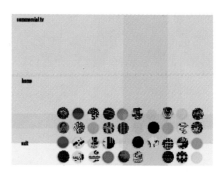

EXIT

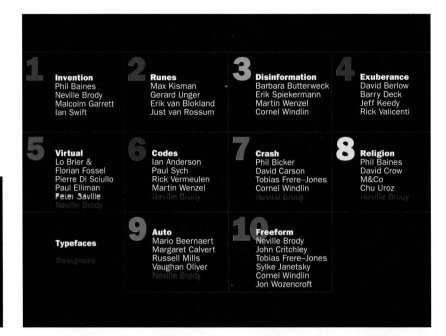

| | | | |
|---|---|---|---|
| **1** **Invention** Phil Baines Neville Brody Malcolm Garrett Ian Swift | **2** **Runes** Max Kisman Gerard Unger Erik van Blokland Just van Rossum | **3** **Disinformation** Barbara Butterweck Erik Spiekermann Martin Wenzel Cornel Windlin | **4** **Exuberance** David Berlow Barry Deck Jeff Keedy Rick Valicenti |
| **5** **Virtual** Lo Brier & Florian Fossel Pierre Di Sciullo Paul Elliman Peter Saville Neville Brody | **6** **Codes** Ian Anderson Paul Sych Rick Vermeulen Martin Wenzel Neville Brody | **7** **Crash** Phil Bicker David Carson Tobias Frere–Jones Cornel Windlin Neville Brody | **8** **Religion** Phil Baines David Crow M&Co Chu Uroz Neville Brody |
| **Typefaces** Designers | **9** **Auto** Mario Beernaert Margaret Calvert Russell Mills Vaughan Oliver Neville Brody | **10** **Freeform** Neville Brody John Critchley Tobias Frere–Jones Sylke Janetsky Cornel Windlin Jon Wozencroft | |

**FUSE CD·ROM 1·10**
Introduction
Index
CD Bonus Fonts
Credits

**3**
**Disinformation**
Barbara Butterweck
Erik Spiekermann
Martin Wenzel
Cornel Windlin

k

**Moonbase Alpha** Cornel Windlin

Moonbase Alpha is an insult to any trained typographer, the mutant cousin of Akzidenz Grotesk with a corrupted DNA. I like it because it has the tacky charm of a mid–seventies science fiction TV series, and because it looks like something straight out of a Letraset catalogue. The typeface is derived from a bitmapped print–out of a sample setting of 6pt Akzidenz, so it more or less designed itself – I simply interpreted what the computer gave me. For this reason, Moonbase works best at large sizes or as an outline, and set very tight without any line–spacing, it creates interesting graphic shapes. Applied in the right way, Moonbase could be used as a pattern generator, but its full potential is not revealed until you've run the whole Mac routine with it. Convert it to paths and mess it up, split it, slant it, stretch it, change the line width, funk it, spike it, remix, rip it up – use it, abuse it, but most of all, have fun with it! Send me the results, show me the damage; but never forget – typography, it really doesn't matter!

**Moonbase Alpha** Cornel Windlin

!"#$%&'()*+,-./0123456789:;<=>?@ABCDEF
GHIJKLMNOPQRSTUVWXYZ[\]_`abcdef
ghijklmnopqrstuvwxyz{|}~ÄÅÇÉÑÖÜáà
âäãåçéèêëíìîïñóòôöõúùûü°¢£§•¶ß®©™´¨
≠ÆØ∞±≤≥¥µ∂∑∏π∫ªºΩæø¿¡¬√ƒ≈∆«»…ÀÃÕŒœ
–—""''÷◊ÿŸ⁄€‹›ﬁﬂ‡·‚„‰ÂÊÁËÈÍÎÏÌÓÔ
ÒÚÛÙıˆ˜¯˘˙˚¸˝˛ˇ

**Moonbase Alpha** Cornel Windlin

**128** Fuse CD 1·10. CD-Rom containing every font from the first ten issues of Fuse. In addition to the fonts (sequences from the animations of each issue are opposite), a multimedia application provides biographies, type layouts and posters.

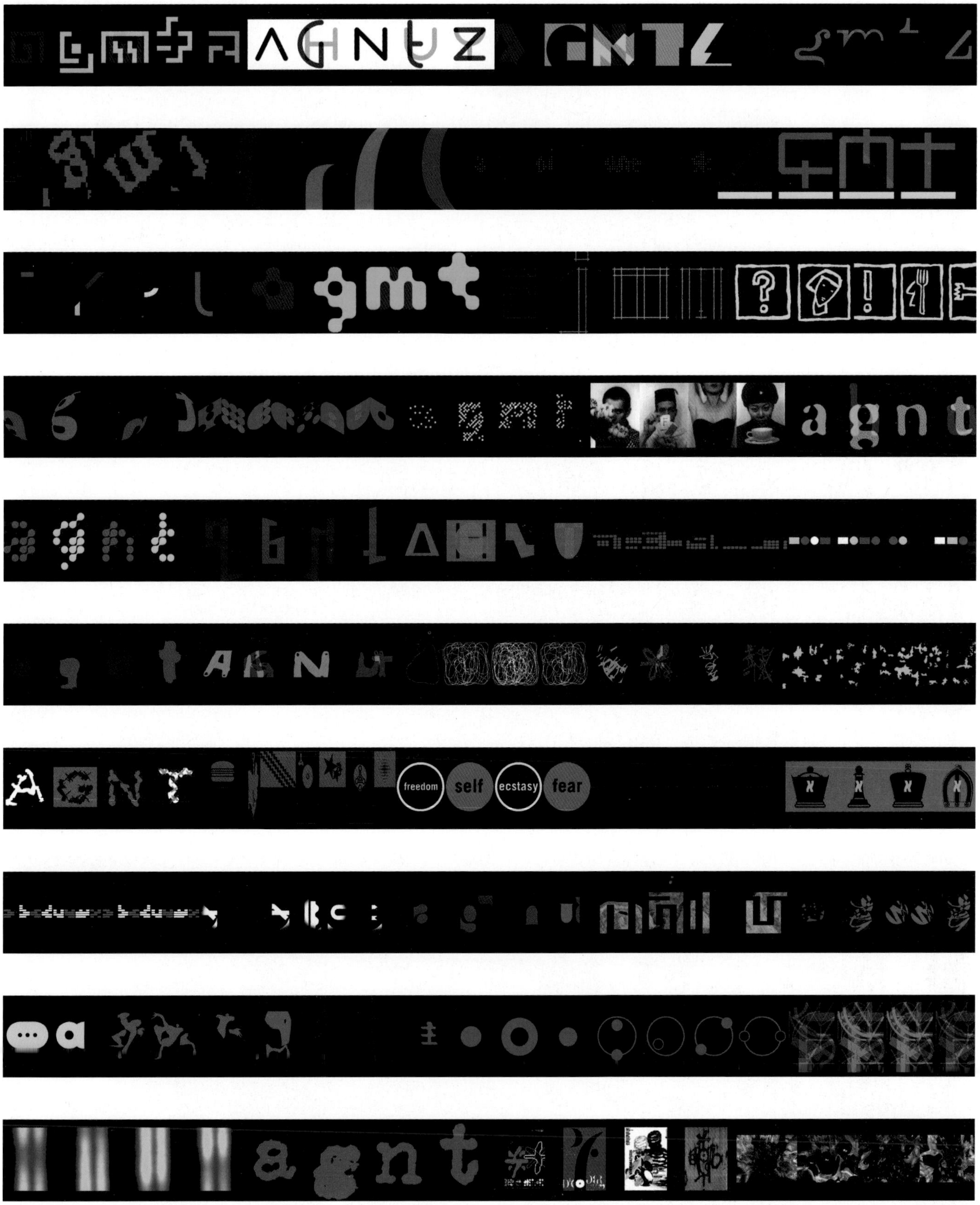
freedom
self
ecstasy
fear

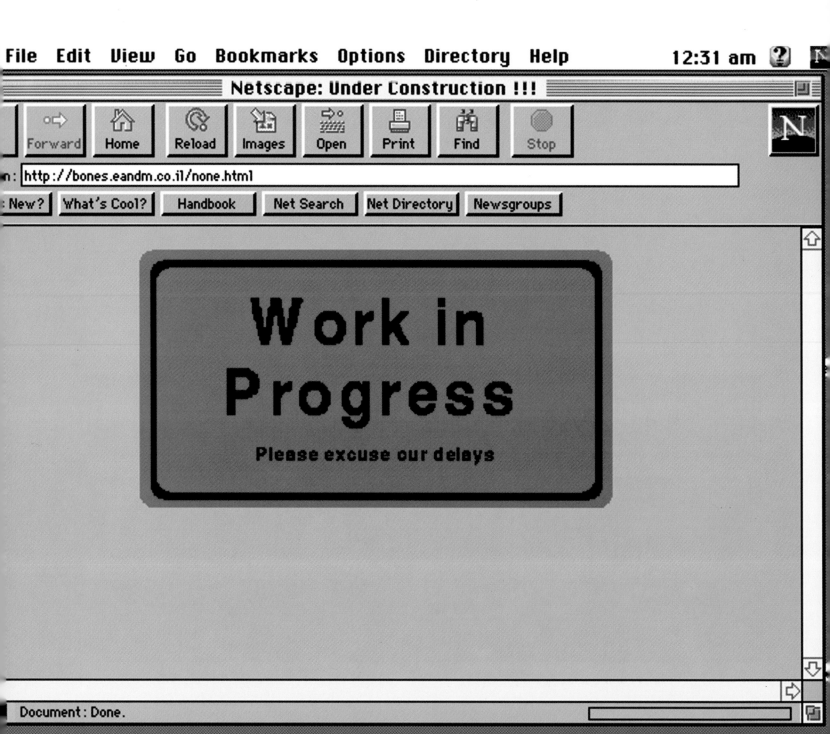

**File    Edit    View    Go    Bookmarks    Options    Directory    Help                    12:31 am**

Netscape: Under Construction !!!

Forward    Home    Reload    Images    Open    Print    Find    Stop

n: http://bones.eandm.co.il/none.html

New?    What's Cool?    Handbook    Net Search    Net Directory    Newsgroups

# Work in Progress

## Please excuse our delays

Document: Done.

**130** Internet pages, May 1996, taken from the
thousands likely to be under construction or
unavailable. The internet browser design is the
property of Netscape Corporation, the most widely
used web browser software. Page designs are partly
determined by end-user system preferences and
calibrations. *Basic screen size 640 x 480 pixels.*

**Even in cyberspace, the vernacular is at home**

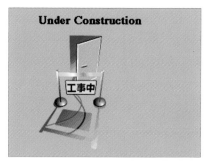
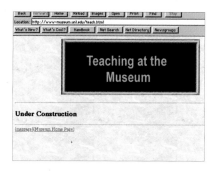

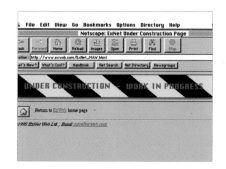
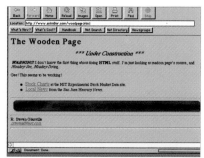
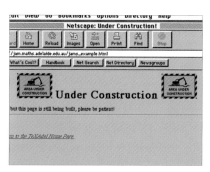

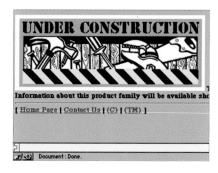
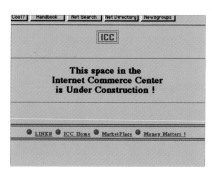
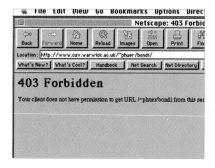

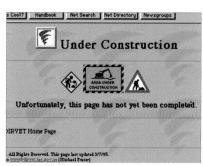

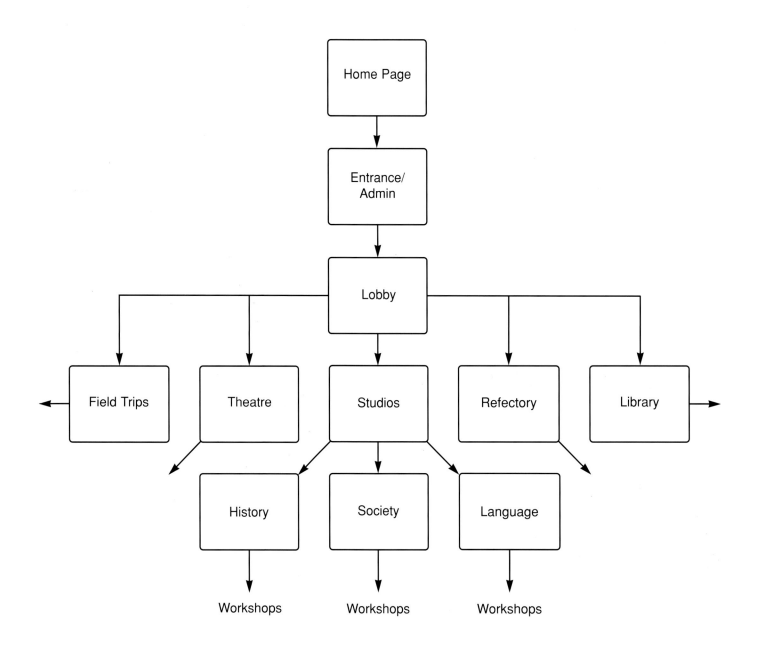

**131** Wild School: University of Nowhere 1996-1999. On-line school of communication design (structure above, interface opposite and following page). Fixed school structure is foregone in favour of allowing participants to find their own way. The school is shaped by its participants, drawing on situations of experiences of the everyday. The only fixed structure is the idea of five themed "workshops" in each of the three departments: society, history and language. Learning resources available across the internet will be drawn into supporting the courses.

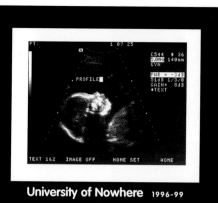

**University of Nowhere** 1996-99

Welcome to the University of Nowhere, itinerant home page and one of the so-called Wild Schools.

This online School of Communication Design offers departments in History, Society and Language, an index of links - each link socialised by everything it touches; an exploring tour and its record.

Go

Just as one excommunicates by naming, the name 'wild' both creates and defines what the scriptural economy situates outside of itself. It is moreover, immediately given its essential predicate:   the wild is transitory; it marks itself (by smudges, lapses, etc) but it does not write itself. It alters a place (it disturbs), but it does not establish a place. Michel de Certeau

Go

Library

Field Trips

Studios

Theatre

Refectory

'Free and easy wandering' it is called by the Chinese sage Chuang Tzu. In free and easy wandering there is only freshness and adventure. Agnes Martin

Go

**Wild School** Version 0.3

Studios

The Exploratorium
Virtual Antarctica (Terraquest)
Subway Navigator
The Met Office
The Virtual Tourist World Map
The New England Aquarium
Ruskin School of Drawing
Virtual Vegas Online
City Net
Kew Gardens

Lobby Studios Library Theatre Refectory

Risks Digest
San Jose Mercury News
Cambridge University Press
Banned Books
City of Bits - William J. Mitchell
The Computer Generated Writing Resource
Noam Chomsky Archive
Pride and Prejudice (Hyper Text)
Complete Works of Shakespeare
Voice of the Shuttle

Lobby  Studios  Field Trips  Theatre Refectory

**Tornado Pilot as an icon
for a Department of History**

Tom Dixon; London, England
Flavia Gandolfo; Lima, Peru
Denise Schmandt-Besserat; Austin, USA
Gavin Turk; London, England
Ceryth Wyn Evans; London England

**Store Detective as an icon
for a Department of Society**

Jane Atfield; London, England
Rosemary Butcher; London, England
Linda van Deursen; Amsterdam, Netherlands
Sue Parker; London, England
Keiko Sawa; Kanazawa, Japan

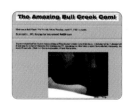

**Computer Programmer as an icon
for a Department of Language**

Ruth Farrington; Oldham, England
Roland François Lack; London, England
James Mason; Taos, USA
Armand Mevis; Amsterdam, Netherlands
Daniel Olsen; Austin, USA

StereoLab
Interactive Star Wars
Jazz Online
Alt.Sex.Movies
World Chess Site
Film Online
Radio Classics
The Electric Brain
Real Audio
Great Globe Gallery

Lobby  Studios  Library  Field Trips  Refectory

CyberEden
The Chocolate Archives
The Internet Lunch Counter
Gourmet Guide
Chile-Heads
PizzaNet
Le Cordon Bleu
Tasty Insect Recipes
Spencer's Beer
Virginia Diner

Lobby  Studios  Library  Field Trips  Theatre

**132** Animated sequence. One of several used throughout an internal conference video for WEA Records. *Approx 30 seconds.*

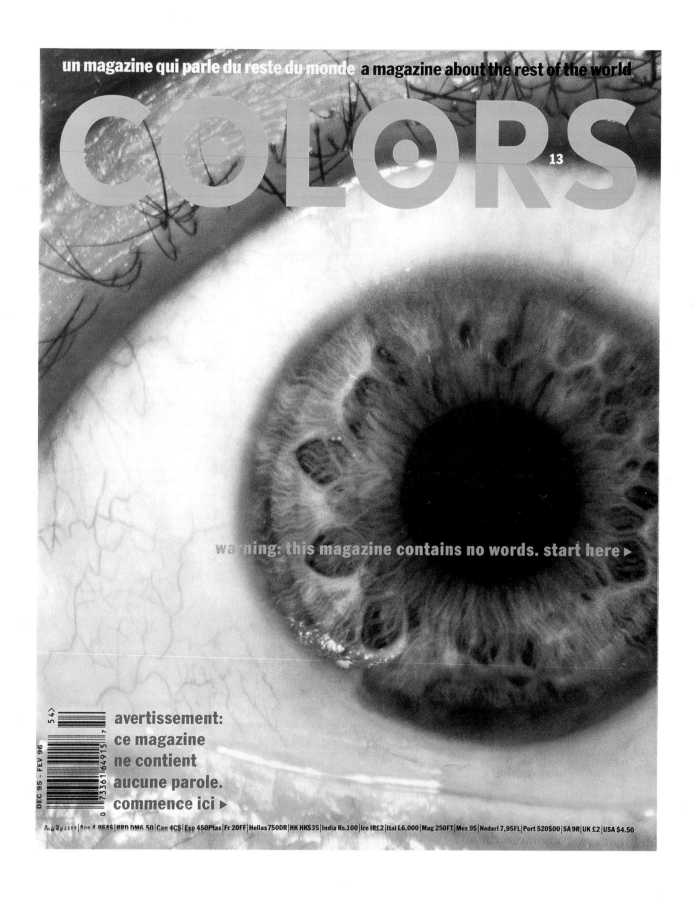

un magazine qui parle du reste du monde **a magazine about the rest of the world**

# COLORS
13

warning: this magazine contains no words. start here ▶

avertissement:
ce magazine
ne contient
aucune parole.
commence ici ▶

DEC 95 - FEV 96

A..iOp....|Aus 4.95A$|BRD DM6.50|Can 4C$|Esp 450Ptas|Fr 20FF|Hellas 750DR|HK HK$35|India Rs.100|ire IR£2|Ital L.6.000|Mag 250FT|Mex 9$|Nederl 7,95FL|Port 520$00|SA 9R|UK £2|USA $4.50

**133** Colors magazine No 13 (here and following three pages), 359 pictures with 442 words of accompanying text. The back cover (page 182) is a collage of an aerial view of Fez, Morocco, with an image of the annual National Day celebrations in Taipei, Taiwan, where posters of the late Chiang Ching Kuo, Son of Chiang Kai Shek, are being carried. 100 pages. *230mm x 288mm.*

PRINTED IN ITALY

**134** Chopstick wrapper for Oki Nami Japanese restaurant. Swan made from folding paper printed with origami instructions. *75mm x 55mm x 40mm, 52 seconds...*

...and counting

76  **Sharon Werner**

77  **Graphic Thought Facility**
designers **Paul Neale**, **Andrew Stevens**

78  **Giovanni Bianco** and **Susanna Cucco**

79  **Giovanni Bianco** and **Susanna Cucco**

80  **Sharon Werner**

81  **Aboud Sodano**

82  **Aboud Sodano**

83  Vernacular supplied by **Susanna Cucco**

84  **Aboud Sodano**

85  **Charles Anderson**

86  **Charles Anderson**

87  **Charles Anderson**

88  **Bruce Mau**

89  **Designer's Republic**

90  **Cornel Windlin**

91  **Fuse**
designer **Cornel Windlin**

92  Vernacular supplied by **Phil Bicker/Village**

93  **Substance**
photograph **Chris Dunlop**

94  **David Crow**

95  Vernacular supplied by **Ian Swift**

96  Vernacular supplied by **Fuel**

97  **The Partners**
partner **Aziz Cami** designer **Greg Quinton**

98  **Nick Livesey**

99  Vernacular supplied by **Phil Bicker/Village**

100  **Nous Travaillons Ensemble**
designer **Alex Jordan**

101  **Saru Brunei Co Ltd**
designer **Gento Matsumoto**

102  **Fuse**
designers **Tom Hingston**, **Jon Wozencroft**

103  Vernacular supplied by **Tom Hingston**

104  **Neville Brody**

105  **Neville Brody**

106  **Paul Elliman**

107  **Peter Grundy**

108  **Frank Heine**

109  **Tobias Frere-Jones**

110  Vernacular supplied by **Tobias Frere-Jones**
digital font by **Tobias Frere-Jones**

111  **Giles Dunn**

112  **Studio Barbara**
designers **Chris Priest**, **Joe Wright**

113  Vernacular supplied by **Sam Chick**

114  **Paul Elliman**

115  Vernacular supplied by **Alex Jordan**

116  **Nous Travaillons Ensemble**
designer **Alex Jordan**

117  **Tycoon Graphics**
designers **Yuuichi Miyashi**, **Naoyuki Suzuki**

118  **Pierre di Scuillo**, **Thomas Hirschhorn**

119  **Bruce Mau**

120  Vernacular supplied by **Paul Elliman**

121  **Andrew Byrom**

122  **Andrew Byrom**

123  **Brian Baderman**

124  **Gary Koepke**
photography **David Byrne**

125  **V23**
designer **Vaughan Oliver** poem **Victoria Mitchell**

126  **Gary Koepke**

127  **Tomato**
creative editor **Tomas Roope/Anti-Rom**

128  **Research Studios** designer/programmer
**Mike Williams** art direction **Simon Staines**

129  **Why Not Associates**

130  Vernacular from the **Internet**

131  **Paul Elliman**

132  **Dylan Kendle**

133  **Tibor Kalman**

134  **Graphic Thought Facility**
designers **Paul Neale**, **Andrew Stevens**

135  Additional photography **Shaun Roberts**

136  **Research Studios** designers **Tom Hingston**,
**John F. McGill**, **Simon Staines**, **Robert Kirk Wilkinson**

Should be in 2D

Should be in 3D

Should be in 4D

Should be somewhere else

76 Sharon Werner

77 Graphic Thought Facility
designers Paul Neale, Andrew Stevens

78 Giovanni Bianco and Susanna Cucco

79 Giovanni Bianco and Susanna Cucco

80 Sharon Werner

81 Aboud Sodano

82 Aboud Sodano

83 Vernacular supplied by Susanna Cucco

84 Aboud Sodano

85 Charles Anderson

86 Charles Anderson

87 Charles Anderson

88 Bruce Mau

89 Designer's Republic

90 Cornel Windlin

91 Fuse
designer Cornel Windlin

92 Vernacular supplied by Phil Bicker/Village

93 Substance
photograph Chris Dunlop

94 David Crow

95 Vernacular supplied by Ian Swift

96 Vernacular supplied by Fuel

97 The Partners
partner Aziz Cami designer Greg Quinton

98 Nick Livesey

99 Vernacular supplied by Phil Bicker/Village

100 Nous Travaillons Ensemble
designer Alex Jordan

101 Saru Brunei Co Ltd
designer Gento Matsumoto

102 Fuse
designers Tom Hingston, Jon Wozencroft

103 Vernacular supplied by Tom Hingston

104 Neville Brody

105 Neville Brody

106 Paul Elliman

107 Peter Grundy

108 Frank Heine

109 Tobias Frere-Jones

110 Vernacular supplied by Tobias Frere-Jones
digital font by Tobias Frere-Jones

111 Giles Dunn

112 Studio Barbara
designers Chris Priest, Joe Wright

113 Vernacular supplied by Sam Chick

114 Paul Elliman

115 Vernacular supplied by Alex Jordan

116 Nous Travaillons Ensemble
designer Alex Jordan

117 Tycoon Graphics
designers Yuuichi Miyashi, Naoyuki Suzuki

120 Vernacular supplied by Paul Elliman

121 Andrew Byrom

122 Andrew Byrom

123 Brian Baderman

124 Gary Koepke
photography David Byrne

125 V23
designer Vaughan Oliver poem Victoria Mitchell

creative editor Tomas Koope/Anti-Rom

128 Research Studios designer/programmer
Mike Williams art direction Simon Staines

129 Why Not Associates

130 Vernacular from the Internet

131 Paul Elliman

132 Dylan Kendle

133 Tibor Kalman

134 Graphic Thought Facility
designers Paul Neale, Andrew Stevens

135 Additional photography Shaun Roberts

136 Research Studios designers Tom Hingston,
John F. McGill, Simon Staines, Robert Kirk Wilkinson

Should be in 2D

Should be in 3D

Should be in 4D

Should be somewhere else

1 Vernacular supplied by **Ian Swift** with thanks to Stef's grandmother

2 Vernacular supplied by **Substance**

3 **Graphic Thought Facility** designers **Paul Neale, Andrew Stevens**

4 **Jayne Alexander**

5 Vernacular supplied by **Phil Bicker/Village**

6 **Emigre** designers **Rudy VanderLans, Zuzana Licko**

7 **Jennifer Morla**

8 **Jennifer Morla**

9 **Giorgio Camuffo**

10 **Graphic Thought Facility** designers **Paul Neale, Andrew Stevens**

11 **Alan Kitching**

12 **Cornel Windlin**

13 **Ian Swift**

14 **Aboud Sodano**

15 Vernacular supplied by **Aboud Sodano**

16 **Designer's Republic** original photograph **Chris Cunningham**

17 **Alyson Waller**

18 **Graphic Thought Facility** designers **Paul Neale, Andrew Stevens** photography **Andrew Penketh**

19 **Carlos Segura**

20 **Substance** designers **Chris Ashworth, Neil Fletcher, Amanda Sissons**

21 **Jon Wozencroft**

22 **Scott Clum**

23 Vernacular supplied by **Scott Clum**

24 **Carlos Segura**

25 **Carlos Segura**

26 **Fuse** designer **Pablo Rovalo Flores**

27 **Carlos Segura**

28 **Alan Fletcher**

29 **Michel Quarez**

30 **Nous Travaillons Ensemble** designer **Alex Jordan**

31 **Nous Travaillons Ensemble** designer **Alex Jordan**

32 **Peret**

33 **Peret**

34 **Why Not Associates** designers **Andrew Altmann, David Ellis, Patrick Morrissey**

35 **Fuel** photography **Matthew Donaldson**

36 Vernacular supplied by **Why Not Associates**

37 **V23** designer **Vaughan Oliver**

38 Vernacular supplied by **Alyson Waller**

39 **Fuel** photography **Annabel Elston, Matthew Donaldson**

40 **Fuel** photography **Annabel Elston**

41 **Substance** photograph **Chris Dunlop**

42 **Cornel Windlin**

43 **Me Company Ltd**

44 Vernacular supplied by **P. Scott Makela**

45 **P. Scott Makela**

46 **P. Scott Makela**

47 **Vince Frost**

48 **Ian Wright, John Critchley**

49 **Anna-Lisa Schönecker**

50 **Leslie Cabarga**

51 **Ian Swift**

52 **Ian Swift**

53 Vernacular supplied by **Ian Swift**

54 **Ian Swift**

55 **Matt Roach**

56 **Norio Nakamura**

57 **Norio Nakamura**

58 **Norio Nakamura, Hiromi Watanabe**

59 **Norio Nakamura**

60 Vernacular supplied by **Linzi Bartolini**

61 **Frogdesign**

62 **Mark Farrow, Mason Wells**

63 **Angus Hyland**

64 Vernacular supplied by **Angus Hyland**

65 **Angus Hyland**

66 **Michael Nash** photography **Matthew Donaldson**

67 **Aboud Sodano**

68 **CDT Design** photography **Uli Weber**

69 Vernacular supplied by **Phil Bicker/Village**

70 **Phil Bicker/Village** photography **David Sims**

71 **Research Studios** designers **Robert Kirk Wilkinson, Neville Brody**

72 **Ben Drury, Will Bankhead**

73 **Jon Wozencroft** photography **Bruce Gilbert**

74 **Jon Wozencroft, Russell Haswell**

75 **Inflate** designer **Michael Sodeau** graphics **Simon Clark**

1   Vernacular supplied by **Ian Swift**
    with thanks to Stef's grandmother

2   Vernacular supplied by **Substance**

3   **Graphic Thought Facility**
    designers **Paul Neale, Andrew Stevens**

4   **Jayne Alexander**

5   Vernacular supplied by **Phil Bicker/Village**

6   **Emigre**
    designers **Rudy Vanderlans, Zuzana Licko**

7   **Jennifer Morla**

8   **Jennifer Morla**

9   **Giorgio Camuffo**

10  **Graphic Thought Facility**
    designers **Paul Neale, Andrew Stevens**

11  **Alan Kitching**

12  **Cornel Windlin**

13  **Ian Swift**

14  **Aboud Sodano**

15  Vernacular supplied by **Aboud Sodano**

16  **Designer's Republic**
    original photograph **Chris Cunningham**

17  **Alyson Waller**

18  **Graphic Thought Facility** designers **Paul Neale,
    Andrew Stevens** photography **Andrew Penketh**

19  **Carlos Segura**

20  **Substance** designers **Chris Ashworth,
    Neil Fletcher, Amanda Sissons**

21  **Jon Wozencroft**

22  **Scott Clum**

23  Vernacular supplied by **Scott Clum**

24  **Carlos Segura**

25  **Carlos Segura**

26  **Fuse**
    designer **Pablo Rovalo Flores**

27  **Carlos Segura**

28  **Alan Fletcher**

29  **Michel Quarez**

30  **Nous Travaillons Ensemble**
    designer **Alex Jordan**

31  **Nous Travaillons Ensemble**
    designer **Alex Jordan**

32  **Peret**

33  **Peret**

34  **Why Not Associates** designers
    **Andrew Altmann, David Ellis, Patrick Morrissey**

35  **Fuel**
    photography **Matthew Donaldson**

36  Vernacular supplied by
    **Why Not Associates**

37  **V23**
    designer **Vaughan Oliver**

38  Vernacular supplied by **Alyson Waller**

39  **Fuel**
    photography **Annabel Elston, Matthew Donaldson**

40  **Fuel**
    photography **Annabel Elston**

41  **Substance**
    photograph **Chris Dunlop**

42  **Cornel Windlin**

43  **Me Company Ltd**

44  Vernacular supplied by **P. Scott Makela**

45  **P. Scott Makela**

46  **P. Scott Makela**

47  **Vince Frost**

48  **Ian Wright, John Critchley**

49  **Anna-Lisa Schönecker**

50  **Leslie Cabarga**

51  **Ian Swift**

52  **Ian Swift**

53  Vernacular supplied by **Ian Swift**

54  **Ian Swift**

55  **Matt Roach**

56  **Norio Nakamura**

57  **Norio Nakamura**

58  **Norio Nakamura, Hiromi Watanabe**

59  **Norio Nakamura**

60  Vernacular supplied by **Linzi Bartolini**

61  **Frogdesign**

62  **Mark Farrow, Mason Wells**

63  **Angus Hyland**

64  Vernacular supplied by **Angus Hyland**

65  **Angus Hyland**

66  **Michael Nash**
    photography **Matthew Donaldson**

67  **Aboud Sodano**

68  **CDT Design**
    photography **Uli Weber**

69  Vernacular supplied by **Phil Bicker/Village**

70  **Phil Bicker/Village**
    photography **David Sims**

71  **Research Studios**
    designers **Robert Kirk Wilkinson, Neville Brody**

72  **Ben Drury, Will Bankhead**

73  **Jon Wozencroft**
    photography **Bruce Gilbert**

74  **Jon Wozencroft, Russell Haswell**

75  **Inflate**
    designer **Michael Sodeau** graphics **Simon Clark**

## BIOGRAPHIES

### Aboud Sodano

Aboud Sodano was formed by the designer Alan Aboud and photographer Sandro Sodano in 1990. In the same year Alan Aboud was appointed art director for Paul Smith Ltd worldwide and the relationship has developed to include all Paul Smith lines. This work has brought recognition from design organizations internationally. The company has also produced high-profile work on HIV/AIDS for the Terrence Higgins Trust, the original work being selected for a citation for typographic excellence by the Type Directors Club, New York. In 1996 it was commissioned to design advertisements for the Vauxhall Omega car campaign and also to produce publicity and advertising for a major photographic retrospective of the work of Nan Goldin at the Whitney Museum of American Art, New York.

### Jayne Alexander

Jayne Alexander studied graphic design at Central Saint Martin's College of Art and Design from 1989 to 1992 and at the Royal College of Art until 1994. With fellow RCA graduate Violetta Boxhill, she then formed the female design studio Alexander Boxhill. One of the aims of the new company is to raise the profile of women in graphic design.

### Charles S. Anderson

Charles S. Anderson founded the Charles S. Anderson Design Company in 1989 in Minneapolis, Minnesota specializing in product design and development, consulting, identity and packaging design. The company has developed a number of products from watches to home furnishings and in 1995 established the CSA Archive, a subsidiary company dealing in original and historic stock illustrations based on its extensive collection of images. Clients include The French Paper Company, Sony, Nike, Levis, Polo Ralph Lauren, Visual Message, Tokyo and Fossil, and the company has also worked on projects with advertising agencies such as Foote, Cone & Belding, DDB Needham and Chiat Day. Its work has been included in exhibitions and permanent collections in galleries and museums in the USA, Europe and Japan.

### Will Bankhead and Ben Drury

Will Bankhead and Ben Drury met at Central Saint Martin's College of Art and Design in London and have been involved with the music industry since their graduation. Initial projects included work for Global Communications/Dedicated Records. Will Bankhead subsequently worked as an A&R for James Lavelle at the Mo' Wax label and produced photography for graphics by Ian Swift. Ben Drury became involved initially with logo work. The two have since collaborated on many Mo' Wax projects.

### Phil Bicker

Phil Bicker originally worked as an illustrator and has an editorial background as the art director of *New Socialist* magazine and *The Face*. Today he is an art director at his London-based company Village. Designer of the Illiterate typeface for *Fuse*, his recent commissions include consultancy for MTV, the Kate Moss book *Kate*, work for *Ray Gun*, and art direction for Jigsaw and Jigsaw Menswear, Bunty Matthias Dance Co. and Wrangler.

### Neville Brody

Neville Brody studied at the London College of Printing, later becoming art director of Fetish Records. In the early 1980s he was art director of *The Face* and *City Limits*, then *Arena*, before setting up his London studio in 1987, now known as Research Studios. For the last seven years he and his team have collaborated with clients including the television stations Première and ORF, the Dutch PTT, the Haus der Kulturen der Welt in Berlin, Parco in Japan and Greenpeace in the UK. Following the publication of *The Graphic Language of Neville Brody* by Thames and Hudson in 1988, an exhibition of his work was held at the Victoria and Albert Museum. Brody helped set up FontWorks (UK), *Fuse* and FontShop International in 1990. He is a partner in the television design company DMC, founded in Vienna. Recent clients include Tokyo-based CD-Rom publishers Digitalogue, *The Guardian* and *The Observer* in London, Sony, United Artists, Armani, Girbaud, Camper and Salomon. *The Graphic Language of Neville Brody 2* was published in 1994.

### Andrew Byrom

Andrew Byrom was born in Liverpool in 1971. After serving an apprenticeship in a shipyard he left to study graphic design at Cumbria College of Art and Design. He later graduated in visual communication from the University of East London and now works with Paul Elliman.

### Leslie Cabarga

Leslie Cabarga has been a professional illustrator since the age of 14 and also produced hand-lettered type from an early age. During the 1990s he used an Apple Macintosh computer in some of his lettering projects and has released a number of fonts, such as BadTyp and Graffiti, through The Font Bureau Inc. Cabarga's work appears regularly in such magazines as *Esquire*, *Fortune*, *Rolling Stone* and *Premiere*. He has produced numerous books on design including *Letterheads: One Hundred Years of Great Design* (Chronicle Books) and *A Treasury of German Trademarks*.

### Aziz Cami/The Partners

Aziz Cami has over 20 years' experience in the design industry. He was one of the founders of The Partners and has held a number of prestigious posts. He was President of Design & Art Direction in Europe from 1992 to 1993 and has served on the DBA Council of Management. His work has earned him numerous awards including four Silver awards from D&AD and *Business* magazine's award for the Best-designed Annual Report. Recent clients include Decca International, Générale des Eaux, Sainsburys and Warner Bros Retail.

### Giorgio Camuffo

Giorgio Camuffo is based in Venice. Much of his work is produced for a variety of cultural institutions such as the Triennale in Milan and the Fortuny Museum in Venice and encompasses signage, catalogues, corporate identity, books and posters. An interest in American graphic design led him to promote a number of exhibitions, most recently staging the "New Pop" exhibition on American illustrators in Venice and Milan.

### CDT

CDT Design, formerly named Carroll, Dempsey and Thirkell after the founding partners, was set up in London in 1979. The consultancy handles a wide range of clients, particularly in the fields of film, leisure and culture, and has received a number of awards in national and international design competitions, notably for its posters for the English National Opera.

### Scott Clum

Scott Clum is the principal of Ride Design, based in Silverton, Oregon. He has produced type, film, video and gallery shows, working for corporations such as Coca Cola and Nike. Ride is probably best known for three magazines: along with Gavin Wilson, Clum publishes *Blur Magazine* which he designs; he developed *Bikini* magazine with Marvin Scott Jarrett, the founder of Ray Gun publishing; and he designs the snowboarding culture magazine *Stick* which he developed with the photographer Trevor Graves. These publications have received awards and media attention internationally and form the basis of talks and lectures by Clum.

### John Critchley

John Critchley graduated from Manchester Polytechnic in 1990 and after a brief period of work at Designer's Republic in Sheffield, joined Neville Brody Studios where he worked on a number of projects including *Fuse*. He left the studio in 1995 to become art director at MTV Europe.

### David Crow

David Crow was born in Galashiels, Scotland in 1962 and graduated in graphic design from Manchester Polytechnic in 1985. He spent three years with Assorted Images in London before becoming the in-house designer for Island Records. After leaving Island, he became freelance, producing work for Rolling Stones Records, RCA, Sony, Virgin Records and the Royal Shakespeare Company. Crow has contributed to a number of exhibitions in the UK and elsewhere. He is subject leader at Liverpool Art School, John Moores University and is a contributor to *Fuse* magazine.

### Giles Dunn

Giles Dunn was born and educated in London, graduating in graphic design from Central Saint Martin's in 1989. After graduating he met Neville Brody and became a member of his studio until 1995. He then moved to New York and set up his own studio which is involved in a wide range of projects in the USA and Europe. He is currently working for SIAC developing future hyper-reality interfaces for the New York Stock Exchange. His work has been widely exhibited and is included in the permanent collections of the Victoria and Albert Museum, London and the Cooper-Hewitt Museum, New York.

### Paul Elliman

Paul Elliman taught at the University of Texas, Austin, before returning to London to set up his own studio. Current projects include a collaboration with Mevis & van Deursen in Amsterdam for the Dutch PTT, and the University of Nowhere internet site, an on-line school of communication design. Since September 1996 he has taught at the Jan van Eyck Academy in Maastricht.

### Emigre

*Emigre* magazine has been a major forum for the investigation of typography and design for over a decade and its central partners are Rudy Vanderlans and Zuzana Licko. Vanderlans was born in The Hague in 1955 where he studied at the Royal Academy of Fine Art. After graduating he worked briefly in Holland then spent some time travelling in the USA. He began graduate studies at the University of California at Berkeley in 1981 and after graduating worked at *The San Francisco Chronicle*. He married Zuzana Licko in 1983. Zuzana Licko was born in Bratislava, Czechoslovakia and emigrated to the USA when she was seven years old. She began to study architecture at Berkeley in 1981, later changing to visual studies. *Emigre* magazine emerged from a travelling exhibition "Dutch Artists on the West Coast". The magazine has been recognized and profiled internationally as a pioneer of digital type and new design.

### Mark Farrow

Mark Farrow was born and studied in Manchester where he began designing for Factory Records and the Haçienda. In 1986 he moved to London where he designed for the Pet Shop Boys and created the look of Deconstruction Records. His work for these and other clients has won numerous awards and has been widely published and exhibited. Mark Farrow Design is based in Clerkenwell, London.

### Pablo Rovalo Flores

Pablo Rovalo Flores was born in 1969 in Mexico City. From 1993 to 1995 he was head of the design direction of the corporate image vice-presidency of Televisa. In 1993 and 1994 he worked on corporate image and internal promotion for channels 2, 5 and 9 in Mexico; and on digital and printed promotion for the 1994 World Cup transmissions. In 1995 he designed the Mexican Yellow Pages for Telmex. He has also worked on images for the Jesuit community in Puebla, and human rights images for the Iberoamericana University. Rovalo Flores dropped out of the graphic design department at the Iberoamericana University with only one subject to finish. He abandoned his career in graphic design after eight years' freelance work in Mexico to travel around Europe, Africa and Asia.

### Frogdesign

Frogdesign was founded in Germany in 1969 and is now an international company with offices in Germany and California. Long renowned in the field of industrial design, the company has integrated this with its graphic design and mechanical engineering capabilities to implement its Integrated Strategic Design. The company has worked with such corporations as Sun Microsystems, Apple Computer, Swatch, Sony and Alessi, amongst many others. Products designed by Frogdesign are in the permanent collections of museums worldwide. In 1992 Hartmut Esslinger and Frogdesign received the inaugural Lucky Strike Designer Award.

### Vince Frost

Vince Frost formed his own consultancy, Frost Design, in 1994. Previously he worked with John Rushworth at Pentagram in London, becoming its youngest ever associate in 1992. He worked as an editorial designer on *P* magazine, a Polaroid publication, whilst still at Pentagram. His involvement in the alternative cultural periodical *Big* brought him international acclaim. A year-long commission art directing the *Independent Magazine* won him numerous awards including recognition from the New York and Tokyo Art Directors Clubs. Frost has continued to work on other projects such as book jackets, music and video titles, corporate identities and typographic animation, and is currently directing sequences for the D&AD award-winners' film.

### Fuel

Fuel was formed by Peter Miles, Damon Murray and Stephen Sorrell in 1991 at the Royal College of Art. The company has worked on many high-profile media campaigns in the last five years for clients including Levis, MTV and *Time Out*.

### Graphic Thought Facility

Graphic Thought Facility are Andy Stevens and Paul Neale, two British graphic designers born in 1966 in Sheffield and Leicestershire respectively. After studying at different colleges, the pair met up at the Royal College of Art and founded the company on graduating in 1990. Neale lectures at Central Saint Martin's College of Art and Design and Stevens lectures at the University of Portsmouth.

### Peter Grundy

Peter Grundy was born in England in 1954 and studied at Bath Academy of Art (from 1973 to 1976) and the Royal College of Art (from 1976 to 1979). He works as a typographer and illustrator with his partner Tilly Northedge. As Peter Grundy Ownworks, he has produced a series of typographic works aimed at bridging the gap between lettering and illustration, an area he calls "iconography".

### Frank Heine

Frank Heine was born in 1964. Following practical courses with a silk-screen printer, a graphics studio and an offset litho printer in 1983, he studied at the Staatliche Akademie der Bildenden Künste in Stuttgart in 1986. He then worked in a graphic design studio for four years, releasing the Remedy font (through Emigre) in 1992, and the Motion font (through Emigre), and the Contrivance, Cutamond, Schablone, Signaler fonts (through Fonthaus) in 1993. In 1994 he founded his own company (together with Lutz Eberie), U.O.R.G., in Stuttgart. His most recent fonts include Chelsea and Instanter (released through Fontshop), Kracklite, Whole Little Universe (through T-26) and in 1995 Amplifier and Indecision (through T-26).

### Tom Hingston

Tom Hingston was born in London in 1973. He studied at the London College of Printing and graduated from Central Saint Martin's College of Art and Design in 1994. He has worked with the designer Paul Allen on various freelance projects for EMI, Katharine Hamnett, Dorado Records and the Blue Note Club, and more recently on a commission for a Foster's Ice billboard. He currently works with Neville Brody at Research Studios and divides his time between his personal work and the studio clients which include Sony, Giorgio Armani and Girbaud. He was recently involved in the design of the title sequences for the Michael Mann film, *Heat*.

### Angus Hyland

Angus Hyland studied at the London College of Printing and graduated in 1988 from the Royal College of Art. Since then he has worked freelance in England and Europe and in collaboration with the designers Louise Cantrill and Silvia Gaspardo-Moro. His work has been published and exhibited both nationally and internationally. He currently runs his own studio from Soho, London.

### Inflate

Inflate was set up by three designers, Nick Crosbie and Michael and Mark Sodeau. Michael Sodeau and Nick Crosbie studied product design at Central Saint Martin's College of Art and Design; Mark Sodeau studied aeronautical engineering and design at City University. After graduating Michael worked for a design consultancy, while Nick studied for a Master's degree at the Royal College of Art. In Autumn 1994 the three partners designed their first collection of products which they have since continued to develop.

### Tobias Frere-Jones

Tobias Frere-Jones is senior managing designer at the Font Bureau Inc. in Boston. In addition to his numerous contributions to the Font Bureau retail library, he has worked for numerous custom clients in the USA and Europe.

### Tibor Kalman

Tibor Kalman was born in Budapest in 1949 and emigrated with his family to the USA in 1956. He studied journalism at New York University and by the end of the 1970s had founded M&Co., working on corporate brochures and signage. A wider range of activities followed involving product design, film and videos. From 1987 to 1991 Kalman was art director of *Artforum* and creative director of *Interview*. From Spring 1991 he worked on *Colors* magazine, moving to Rome for a full-time commitment to the project until the 13th issue. He has now moved back to New York where he plans to become involved in television and other media. Several museums have archives of Kalman's work, including the Cooper-Hewitt Museum, New York, the Victoria and Albert Museum, London and the Stedelijk Museum, Amsterdam.

### Dylan Kendle

Dylan Kendle was born in 1971 and graduated from Camberwell College of Art in 1994. After graduating he worked at Tomato until February 1996. His clients currently include Nike, Smith Kline Beecham, I.C.A., Junior Boys Own, WEA Records and East West Records. In 1996 he was nominated for an award from the Tokyo Type Directors Club.

**Alan Kitching**

Alan Kitching finished his apprenticeship as a compositor in 1961 and by 1964 had established the Experimental Printing Workshop with Anthony Froshaug which exhibited its first year's work at the Institute of Contemporary Art in London. Kitching formed Omnific Studios Partnership with Derek Birdsall in 1978 and later established a letterpress studio, founding The Typography Workshop in 1989. He has been the subject of many articles and in 1994 was appointed a Royal Designer for Industry. He is associated with many university art schools in the UK through typography lecturing and his letterpress workshops.

**Gary Koepke**

Gary Koepke first gained recognition as the art director of *Musician* magazine in the USA from 1984 to 1988. In 1988 he founded Koepke Design Group specializing in advertising and design. He has since designed and directed many magazines including the second issue of *Colors* magazine, and created *World Tour* magazine for Dun & Bradstreet software. He has recently designed *Strange Ritual*, a book by David Byrne, and *SoHo Journal*, an annual to raise money for the homeless. Currently Koepke is the editor of *Big* magazine and an art director at Wieden & Kennedy in Portland, Oregon. His work has been recognized by the Art Directors Club of New York and the Society of Publication Designers in the USA. It has been exhibited internationally and profiled in publications worldwide.

**Nick Livesey**

Nick Livesey was born in 1972 and studied at the Royal College of Art. He has worked with Aboud Sodano and Why Not Associates and specializes in film, photography, typography, three-dimensional work and promotional material. His work has been included in exhibitions at the British Film Institute (Cannes, 1995) and the Royal Academy of Arts (1996).

**Gento Matsumoto**

Gento Matsumoto is a graduate of the Kuwazawa School of Design, Japan. Since 1990 his output as a designer has been as the founding principal of the Saru Brunei company. The company's work is focused mainly on art direction, poster and logo design and the production of fonts. Over the past decade Matsumoto's work has received recognition in Japan and internationally.

**Bruce Mau**

Bruce Mau was born in Canada in 1960. He studied at the Ontario College of Art, leaving prior to graduation to work for the Fingers design group. He then worked at Pentagram in the UK, returning to Toronto in 1983 to help found the Public Good design company which mainly produces work for the health industry. In 1987 he began to design the *Zone* series of volumes of contemporary philosophy. As the principal of Bruce Mau Design he has been a Creative Director of *ID* magazine (USA) and has engaged in two extensive collaborations with architects. He has produced signage, books and exhibition material for the Canadian-born architect Frank Gehry and collaborated on the *S,M,L,XI* project with the Dutch architect Rem Koolhaas.

**John F. McGill**

John F. McGill was born in 1961 and graduated from the Central School of Art and Design in 1983. He has worked on a variety of projects including record sleeves for Motorhead and Van Morrison, titles for the films *Stormy Monday* and *Straight To Hell*, conference material for the Institute of Practitioners in Advertising and the DTI, and a range of work concerning environment, development and health issues for The Panos Institute and their associated photographic library Panos Pictures. Since 1992 he has also worked as a part-time lecturer in Computer-Aided Design at Staffordshire University.

**Me Company**

Me Company, based in London, has established itself over the last decade as an innovative design resource. The group is associated with a number of clients for whom it has produced some well-known images. Its most renowned collaboration is with the singer Bjork which has pushed digitally-based print into new modes of expression.

**Michael Nash Associates**

Michael Nash Associates is the partnership of Anthony Michael and Stephanie Nash, both of whom studied at Saint Martin's School of Art. After graduating in 1981, Stephanie Nash worked at Island Records for artists such as Grace Jones and The Waterboys. Anthony Michael worked with Circa Records for artists such as Neneh Cherry and Massive Attack. After forming Michael Nash they continued to work on music industry projects for Seal, INXS and Del Amitri. Their range of clients has expanded to include, amongst others, fashion industry clients such as Jasper Conran, Issey Miyake and Patrick Cox. Michael Nash has received recognition for its projects including a European Art Directors Award, the New York Festivals Grand Award for Graphic Design and a D&AD Gold (1993) for the food packaging the company implemented for the department store Harvey Nichols, and D&AD Silvers (1994, 1995).

**Jennifer Morla**

Jennifer Morla is president and creative director of Morla Design, San Francisco. She has worked on varied projects from annual reports to music videos and has received over 500 awards. In addition to teaching at California College of Arts and Crafts, she paints, sculpts, and creates site-specific installations. Her work forms part of the permanent collection of the Museum of Modern Art, San Francisco and the Library of Congress, and has been exhibited in Paris and Berlin. The most recent international exhibition of her work was in Osaka, Japan.

**Norio Nakamura**

Norio Nakamura was born in 1967 in Kanagawa Prefecture, Kawasaki City, Japan. In 1990 he graduated from the Nihon University College of Art and began work at the CBS Sony Group where he is currently art director and graphic designer for the planning and development division of Sony Music Entertainment. From 1992 to 1994 Nakamura received the Mainichi Newspaper Advertisement Award for Achievement in Design. He has also been twice awarded the Mainichi Newspaper Advertisement Award Grand Prix.

**Nous Travaillons Ensemble**

Nous Travaillons Ensemble is the collective signature of a group of independent graphic designers created in 1991. The group was co-founded by Alex Jordan (born in 1947) and Ronit Meirovitz (born in Israel in 1954), both of whom had previously worked at Grapus. The pair have since been joined by Jean-Marc Brétégnier, Isabelle Jégo and Nathalie Minne. The group is well known for its work in book and poster design, and received first prize for political and social posters at the Festival d'Affiches de Chaumont in 1995.

**Vaughan Oliver**

Vaughan Oliver graduated from Newcastle upon Tyne Polytechnic in 1979, working first at Benchmark and then at Michael Peters. During this time he met Ivo Watts-Russell, founder of the 4AD record label, and began to produce freelance work for the label. His relationship with the company has been both freelance and in-house. The majority of his output has been within the music industry but he has also produced posters, television titles, book jackets and magazine design for Ray Gun Publishing. His work has been exhibited regularly in Japan, Europe and the USA.

**Peret**

Peret (Pedro Torrent) was born in 1945 in Barcelona where, apart from several years in the 1970s when he worked in Paris, he has always been based. Peret has worked on a wide range of projects encompassing magazines, advertising, television and posters, and he has exhibited both collectively and individually throughout the world. His work has been seen yet more widely in stamps he designed for the Barcelona Olympics and the Seville Expo. Clients include La Vanguardia, Ogilvy and Mather, Pressalit and Swatch.

**Michel Quarez**

Michel Quarez was born in Damascus in 1938. He studied at the School of Fine Arts, Bordeaux, then in Paris and later in Warsaw. He has a long track-record of producing posters and poster art and is at present designing posters for the International Exhibition of Architecture and Music.

**Matt Roach**

Matt Roach was born in Suffolk, England in 1970. He studied architecture for a year before taking a graphics degree at the London College of Printing. Prior to graduation he worked on various student magazines and other projects, eventually assisting the Art Director of *Dazed and Confused* magazine. While at *Dazed and Confused* he set up a freelance design agency (Artificial Sweetener) and he continued working with both until 1995 when he was asked to art direct the new magazine *True*. Whilst art directing *True* Roach set up Astrosuzuki and has undertaken work for various companies including Sony, EMI, Polydor and Island. Current work includes projects for Sony, MTV Europe and Storm.

**Shaun Roberts**

Shaun Roberts was born in 1960 in Leeds. Before commencing a career as a freelance photographer in London, he assisted many photographers in order to gain technical knowledge. He currently specializes in manipulated imagery for magazines and corporate brochures, and recently completed a degree course at Central Saint Martin's College of Art and Design. His interest in film and screen graphics has led to work on title sequences and commercials.

**Anna-Lisa Schönecker**

Anna-Lisa Schönecker was born in 1967 in Germany. She studied product and graphic design at the Fachhochschule Niederrhein Krefeld, at the same time working in film and television. After graduating she was awarded a scholarship and continued her studies at the Royal College of Art, London, focusing on the interrelationship between product and graphic design and audio/visual representation. She currently works at Pentagram Design, London, on both domestic and international projects. Her work has been published in *Blueprint* magazine, London, *Typographies*, Tokyo and *Page* magazine, Hamburg.

**P. Scott Makela**

P. Scott Makela was born in Minnesota, USA in 1960. He studied at the University of Minnesota, Minneapolis College of Art and Design and Cranbrook Academy of Art, Michigan. His output ranges from product design to video design direction but his main area of activity is digital typography and graphic design. In three successive Makela companies over the last decade he has produced work for corporate clients, publications and public bodies, in music, fashion, education, architecture and other fields. Makela has been awarded many honours, such as the Sony International Electronics Award. He has taught at design schools in the USA and internationally. With his wife, Laurie Haycock, he currently heads the 2D design course at Cranbrook. He is also in partnership with the director Jeffrey Plansker.

**Carlos Segura**

Carlos Segura was born in Cuba and moved to the USA in 1965. He lived first in Miami, where he was involved in the music industry as a drummer and public relations manager, and was then employed in New Orleans on the strength of the work he had produced during this time. Since 1980 he has been based in Chicago, working initially for several advertising agencies such as DDB Needham and Masteller. He founded Segura Inc. and his digital type foundry [T-26] in 1991.

**Simon Staines**

Simon Staines was born in England in 1967 and graduated from the London College of Printing in 1989. Working first at *Arena* and *The Face* magazines he then joined Neville Brody working with clients which included Closed, Fiorucci, *The Guardian* and *Observer* newspapers, Ikea, Actuel, AGFA, ORF and Premiere Television. Now an art director at the recently formed Research Studios he has just completed the art direction and design of all the interactive sequences and computer screens in the films *Mission Impossible* and *Hackers*, and title sequences for *Heat* and *Secret Agent*. He is currently working with Giorgio Armani and Girbaud.

**Studio Barbara**

Studio Barbara is the collaboration of Chris Priest and Joe Wright and dates from October 1995. Clients include Saatchi & Saatchi, Virgin Records and Ogilvy and Mather. Chris Priest studied at the Bournville School of Art and Central Saint Martin's College of Art and Design. After graduating in 1989 he worked at Why Not Associates in London until 1993, then freelanced until the formation of Studio Barbara. A former sportsman and musician, he has lectured at the Watford School of Art and is now concentrating on animation and film work. Joe Wright attended Camberwell School of Art and Central Saint Martin's College of Art and Design. After graduating in 1993 he moved to New York to work for Arnell Bickford Associates. He then returned to the UK and freelanced for clients such as MTV and Diesel Clothing until the formation of Studio Barbara. He lectures at Camberwell School of Art.

**Substance**

Substance was founded in 1995 by Chris Ashworth, Amanda Sissons and Neil Fletcher. Previously Chris Ashworth had worked as a freelance designer at MTV Europe, producing the first MTV European Music Awards Brochure with John Warwicker and Simon Taylor at Tomato. Amanda Sissons completed a degree in graphic and media design at the London College of Printing in 1995, and Neil Fletcher ran his own design partnership in North Yorkshire. Substance's client list includes MTV Europe, Image Bank, *Creative Review*, NTL Telecommunications, Cornerhouse Publications, Sheffield University and WEA Records, amongst others. The company currently designs and art directs Ray Gun Publishing's UK magazine *Blah Blah Blah*. Other work includes a corporate identity for Sugar Records and a 48-page booklet for photographers. Before forming Substance, the partners produced *Interference*, a personal collection of photographs on the subject of surveillance, for John Holden.

**Ian Swift**

Ian Swift studied graphic design at Manchester Polytechnic and in his final year became a designer on *Fresh* magazine. This led to work on *The Face* as a junior designer until 1988 when he left the magazine to become a senior designer at Neville Brody's studio. After leaving the studio he briefly took over the art direction of *Arena* before moving to the lesser-known magazine *Straight No Chaser*. This work brought him widespread recognition and art direction with record companies such as B&W Music, Source, Talkin' Loud and Mo' Wax. His work forms part of the latest Foster's advertisements. He produces his own fanzine, *Command Z*, and a range of clothing, and is involved in other fashion-related work.

**Tycoon Graphics**

Tycoon Graphics is the company at the centre of a collaboration between two Japanese designers, Yuuichi Miyashi and Naoyuki Suzuki. It was established in 1991 when both designers had returned to Japan after a year's residence in New York. Yuuichi Miyashi was born in 1964 in Tokyo. Naoyuki Suzuki was born in the same year and is a graduate of the Tokyo Art School.

**Alyson Waller**

Alyson Waller was born in 1973 and studied graphic design at Kingston University, graduating in 1995. She has freelanced for Island Records and Tenth Planet, and is currently working at Research Studios.

**Mason Wells**

Mason Wells graduated from Gwent College of Higher Education in 1992 then attended Central Saint Martin's College of Art and Design. From 1993 to 1995 he worked for Cartlidge Levene where he was involved in projects for the Design Museum and the South Bank Centre. He then moved to Mark Farrow Design, working on projects for clients such as the Pet Shop Boys, and is currently working at North with Simon Browning and Sean Perkins.

**Sharon Werner**

Sharon Werner is the principal of Werner Design Werks Inc. which she set up in 1992. Prior to this she was a senior designer at Duffy Design Group. Since she started to work independently her clients have included Bloomingdales, MTV Network, Chronicle Books, Target Stores and the College of Visual Arts. She has received awards from the American Center for Design, New York Art Directors and D&AD in the UK. Her wide-ranging work is included in the permanent collection of, amongst others, the Library of Congress, the Cooper-Hewitt Museum, New York and the Victoria and Albert Museum, London.

**Why Not Associates**

Andrew Altmann and David Ellis formed Why Not Associates in 1987 after graduating from the Royal College of Art. Their innovative approach has led to a wide range of clients including the Green Party, the Foreign and Commonwealth Office, Smirnoff Vodka, Branson Coates Architecture, the Pompidou Centre in Paris and Hull City Council. The company is active in most forms of design for print and regularly works with original Why Not collaborator Howard Greenhalgh at Why Not Films. Its work has been exhibited internationally and the principals contribute to conferences around the world.

**Robert Kirk Wilkinson**

Robert Kirk Wilkinson was born in Bradford in 1970. He studied graphic design at Central Saint Martin's College of Art and Design and in 1994 joined Research Studios where he has worked on a variety of projects.

**Mike Williams**

Mike Williams was born in Hobart, Tasmania. After studying Information Systems at Manchester University, he worked for five years on interactive educational and training systems for museums and coporate clients such as Ford, The Bank of England, IBM and Philips. In 1993 he was sponsored by the games company Electronic Arts to study Interactive Multimedia at the Royal College of Art. He joined Research Studios in 1994. During his time at the studio he has worked on interactive sequences for the films *Mission Impossible* and *Hackers*, the title sequences for *Secret Agent* and *Heat* and the CD-Rom Fuse CD 1•10.

**Cornel Windlin**

Cornel Windlin was born in Switzerland in 1964 and studied graphic design and visual communication at the Schule für Gestaltung in Lucerne where he was taught by Hans-Rudolf Lutz. In 1987 he began working with Neville Brody and moved to the UK to join his studio on a permanent basis a year later. In order to learn more about magazine design he left the Brody Studio to join *The Face* in 1990. He then set up his own studio and has since lived and worked as a freelance art director/designer in London and Zurich.

**Jon Wozencroft**

Jon Wozencroft set up the audio-visual publishers Touch after graduating from the London College of Printing in 1982. He has worked with Neville Brody and his studio since it was set up in 1987, and wrote the two books on Brody's work published by Thames and Hudson, as well as collaborating on Brody exhibitions, the *Fuse* series, and work for Greenpeace, the Body Shop, *The Guardian* and the pop. group Wire. He contributes regularly to *New Scientist* magazine. Between 1992 and 1994 he assisted in the organization of the new teaching programme in graphic design at Central Saint Martin's College of Art and Design, and is currently the main tutor for the Master of Art course in Interactive Multimedia at the Royal College of Art.

**Ian Wright**

Ian Wright has been working as an illustrator for over fifteen years. During this time he has produced record sleeves for a diverse range of artists including Madness (1980s) and On-U sound (1990s), and has worked for several publications in Europe and the USA. Known for his innovative use of hi-tech equipment, he recently collaborated with Blink Productions on the "Hell Without" Foster's Ice cinema commercial and is currently a visiting lecturer at Camberwell College of Art.